SOCIAL SCIENCE STUDIES, No. 14

The Andros Islanders

The Andros Islanders

A Study of Family Organization in the Bahamas

by

Keith F. Otterbein

UNIVERSITY OF KANSAS PUBLICATIONS

Lawrence, 1966

To My Parents

Ralph F. and Mary B. Otterbein

Preface

NEW WORLD NEGRO family organization has been characterized as maternal (Frazier 1939; King 1945), mother-centered (Parsons 1949: 181), matri-centered (Firth and Djamour 1956: 41), consanguineal (Solien 1959), or matri-focal (R. T. Smith 1956). These terms, which stress the importance of the mother's role in the family, refer to what are believed by social scientists to be the three primary distinguishing features of New World Negro family organization: close affective ties between mothers and their children, domestic units dominated by females, and high frequencies of female-headed households. This book describes such a family organization.

In order to investigate New World Negro family organization, I undertook during the summer of 1959 a field study of a community in the Bahama Islands. The Bahamas were my choice because practically no anthropological field work, except for the collecting of folktales (Parsons 1916; Crowley 1956a), had been conducted in the islands. Of the twenty-two inhabited islands in the Bahamas, I selected Andros (see Map 1), for there was available a collection of over a hundred folktales (Parsons 1916), which provided a limited amount of background information on the native way of life in Andros Island. Another reason for this selection was its reputation as the most "primitive" (Mitchell 1958: 178), backward, or underdeveloped of the islands. I hoped that where little social change had occurred the chances of finding cultural retentions or survivals would be increased, for according to Puckett (1926: 69), "The rural Negro is less exposed to contact with modern civilization and his beliefs consequently change more slowly and give us an index of attitudes of the past." Since a luxurious resort had been built by Axel Wenner-Gren at Fresh Creek in northern Andros, this part of the island would presumably show the greatest amount of social change; therefore the community I chose for intensive analysis was in southern Andros.

During the summer of 1959 I lived in Long Bay Cays, a settlement district which extends from the south bank of the Southern Bight south along the eastern coast of Andros for a distance of eight and one-half miles (see Map 2). The district is composed of seven villages—from north to south, Drigg's Hill, Long Bays, Congo Town, Motion Town, Duncombe Coppice, High Rock, and The Bluff. I lived in Motion Town, the administrative and communication center of Long Bay Cays. Using the method of participant observation, I gathered data on all aspects of social life. However, I spent the largest part of my time collecting information on family life. I returned to Long Bay Cays in the summer of 1961 and stayed in Congo Town. During this period I conducted a detailed census of each household in Long Bay Cays, Congo Town, Motion Town, and Duncombe Coppice (the Appendix contains a copy of the census outline), choosing these four villages for intensive analysis because they were the villages in which I had made the most friends during my first field trip; for this reason I believed that census reports taken in these villages would have greater reliability than those taken in Drigg's Hill, High Rock, or The Bluff. My reason for not extending the survey to include these three villages was a practical one: the distance between villages meant that I would have had to shift residence twice during the summer of 1961—moves which would have made it difficult to establish and maintain rapport with the villagers. This second summer field trip also provided the opportunity to fill gaps in the previously collected ethnographic data.

Investigation of New World Negro family organization in recent years has assumed an important place in the growing body of literature on social structure. In addition to their purely ethnographic value, at least two conceptual or methodological contributions have stemmed from these studies. The first of these has been the recognition that the field researcher should focus on the household (or, more precisely, the types of households in the society or community under investigation), a localized or residential group, rather than upon the family, a kinship group. This shift in focus was initially not intentional. Researchers undertaking field studies in the West Indies in the early 1950's (Clarke 1957; R. T. Smith 1956) were forced, by the great variability in household composition within a community and from community to community, to conduct household censuses and to analyze their census data before they attempted to describe the family as a kinship group. Once this shift was made, there was a vast improvement in the quality of monographs. One only needs to compare Henriques' study of the Jamaican family (1953) and its inadequate discussion of family types with Clarke's analysis of Jamaican household types in order to understand the transformation in quality that resulted from this shift in focus. Recent investigators have been quick to realize the significance of the new point of view (Solien 1960). Perhaps the most important study using the household-type approach is M. G. Smith's analysis of five communities in Grenada, Carriacou, and Jamaica (1962a). Other researchers have found the approach useful for studying family organization outside the New World (Otterbein 1963b).

The second contribution, closely related to the first, is the realization that statistical norms, derived largely from census reports, should take precedence over jural rules (i.e., the legal aspects of kinship relations) in the analysis of social structure. (The conceptual distinction between statistical norms and jural rules comes from E. R. Leach's study of Pul Eliya, a village in Ceylon [1961].) I reached the conclusion, after my first summer field trip to the Bahamas, that by studying only kinship relations without first analyzing census data one cannot understand how the family organization of a New World Negro community is articulated

ix

with the rest of the social system. Other researchers, most notably M. G. Smith (1962a), were drawing a similar conclusion. Even though I do not agree with Smith's extreme statement of the position (1962a: 6-9, 20-23)—namely, that principles of social structure are to be derived from quantitative data alone—I do agree with his basic approach.

The following analysis of the family organization of the Andros Islanders utilizes these two methodological contributions. The household is the basic unit of analysis, and when possible I have used statistical data in the deriving of social patterns. The mating and domestic system of the Andros Islanders is the primary concern of this study. Analysis of household composition made it manifestly clear that the courtship and mating system had a strong influence on the occurrence and frequency of household types. In turn, certain economic and demographic factors are chiefly responsible for the mating system. On the other hand, household composition was found to be the primary determinant of interpersonal relationships. These four aspects of the family organization of Long Bay Cays are described in the following order: economic and demographic conditions, the courtship and mating system, household composition, and interpersonal relationships.

I am indebted to a number of individuals who have assisted me at various stages in research and in preparation of this manuscript. Professor George P. Murdock guided the research while I was a graduate student at the University of Pittsburgh. Several other faculty members, especially Professors Fred Adelman, John P. Gillin, Edward A. Kennard, and David Landy, were of assistance in guiding the research in its earlier stages. Four of my fellow students—I. R. Buchler, Claire F. Horton, William P. Mitchell, and Aura Watson—spent many hours discussing with me the subject of Caribbean family organization. Special mention must be made of Professor Cyrus J. Sharer of Villanova University, wh provided me with a general orientation to the Bahamas prior to my first field trip and who since then has aided me in many ways, including a critical reading of the first section of Chapter I. I am grateful to *Social and Economic Studies* for permission to reprint tables and text material from two articles (Otterbein 1963a: 78-83; Otterbein 1964a: 282-301). The maps were drawn by Craig Hartline. My wife, Charlotte Swanson Otterbein, and the editorial staff of the University of Kansas Press have spent many hours editing the manuscript.

Contents

	Preface	vii
I.	The Setting: Long Bay Cays	1
II.	Courtship, Marriage, and Childbirth	33
III.	The Mating System	67
IV.	The Household	85
V.	Interpersonal Relationships	117
VI.	Conclusion	136
	References	140
	Appendix	146
	Index	149

ILLUSTRATIONS

Main dock at Motion Town	*facing*	32
A "smock-boat" pulled up on shore for repairs	"	32
Anglican cemetery in Motion Town	"	33
Post office-courthouse in Motion Town	"	33
The procession leaving the church after a wedding	"	48
Anglican church in Motion Town	"	48
Limestone house with unfinished walls	"	49
Limestone house with the walls plastered over with cement	"	49

MAPS

1.	ANDROS ISLAND AND ITS RELATIONSHIP TO OTHER ISLANDS IN THE BAHAMAS	7
2.	SKETCH-MAP OF LONG BAY CAYS	8
3.	SKETCH-MAP OF LONG BAYS	15
4.	SKETCH-MAP OF CONGO TOWN	16
5.	SKETCH-MAP OF MOTION TOWN	19
6.	SKETCH-MAP OF DUNCOMBE COPPICE	20

Chapter I

The Setting: Long Bay Cays

GEOGRAPHY

THE BAHAMA ISLANDS, a chain of islands, reefs, and cays lying southeast off the Florida coast, extend "over an area of seven hundred and sixty miles, from 20° 56′ to 27° 22′ North latitude and between 72° 40′ and 79° 20′ West longitude" (Mosely 1926: 7). The largest islands in the group are rimmed with sandy beaches and coconut groves. Running the length of these islands are low-lying hills which seldom exceed a height of 100 feet (Edwards 1895: 13). Pine forests grow on many of the ridges. The Bahamas have a subtropical oceanic climate. The annual mean daily temperature is 77° F., the mean for the coldest month (February) being 71° F. and the mean for the warmest (August) 83° F. (Fassig 1905: 116). Rainfall, concentrated in the late summer months, averages about 50 inches per year at Nassau (1905: 117).

Andros, the largest island in the Bahamas, is approximately 100 miles long and 40 miles wide. A rocky ridge, composed of oölitic limestone, extends along the east coast, except at the extreme southern end of the island. This ridge supports a hardwood growth called the "coppet," and a pine forest, known locally as the "pine-yard," lies west of this growth. A mangrove swamp, called the "swash," makes up the west coast of the island; in contrast, the eastern shore is bordered by sandy beaches and coconut trees. Between the "pine-yard" and the "swash" are level prairie-like stretches resembling savannas (Northrop 1910b: 121-22). The villages lie between the coconut groves and the hilly region. Hardly any soil is to be found on the island; this fact is probably "the natural result of a complete lack of insoluble constituents in the limestone" (Newell *et al.* 1951: 10).

1

A barrier reef, which extends out into the ocean for a distance of about two miles, runs along the east coast of Andros, so that vessels drawing more than six feet of water cannot approach close to the island. Along the west coast is the Great Bahama Bank, where at one time was located the West Indies' largest sponging ground, known as the "Mud." The water here is so shallow that even small vessels cannot approach within miles of the shore. The island is divided into sections by three channels, five to twenty-five miles wide. These passages, which are dotted with innumerable small islands, are known as the North Bight, Middle Bight, and Southern Bight (Mosely 1926: 64).

HISTORY

The Bahamas were discovered by Europeans in 1492, when Columbus made his first landing in the West Indies on San Salvador, or Watlings Island. The aboriginal population—the Lucayan Indians—was forcibly transported to Hispaniola and Cuba by the Spaniards to work in mines, and in twenty-five years the islands were depopulated (Peggs 1959: 6). During the latter half of the seventeenth century, English settlers, who brought with them their Negro slaves, colonized the islands. By 1773 the population, which totaled approximately 4,000, was composed of equal numbers of whites and Negroes (Sharer 1955: 33). Between 1783 and 1785 many Loyalists who had been expelled from the American colonies began immigrating to the islands with their slaves (Siebert 1913). These slaves had originally been transported to the New World from West Africa during the eighteenth century to work on plantations which specialized in raising cotton. This influx to the Bahamas increased the number of whites to approximately 3,000 and the number of Negroes to approximately 6,000 (Sharer 1955: 35).

Plantations on the "Cotton Islands." Most of the slave plantations established by the Loyalists in the Bahamas were on the

2

"Cotton Islands"—Cat Island, the Exumas, Long Island, Crooked Island, Watlings Island, and Rum Cay. At first they were successful economic enterprises; however, after 1800 the production of cotton on these islands declined (McKinnen 1804: 192-93) because the slash-and-burn technique for preparing fields prior to planting was injurious to the soil (Sharer 1955: 37; Mooney 1905: 172).

Information on plantation life is limited. Farquharson's journal for 1831-32, the diary of a slaveowner on Watlings Island, provides some data on agriculture and technology. Peggs' introduction to the journal states that "the chief crop of the Estate appears to have been Guinea corn, known elsewhere as sorghum. A number of varieties are mentioned: early corn, late corn, close-head corn. This was chiefly a subsistence crop, grown as food for slaves (vide 'the Saturday allowance')" . . . (Farquharson 1957: iv). Other crops in their approximate order of importance were Indian corn, pigeon peas, cowpeas, black-eyed peas, yams, sweet potatoes, snap beans, castor beans (for oil), cabbage, and pumpkins.

In order to present a summary picture of slash-and-burn agriculture and house-building, Peggs quotes liberally from the original in the following passages (Farquharson 1957: vi-vii):

New land had to be prepared: first, "cutting lines" followed by "falling (felling) new ground" ie. the time-honoured Bahamian procedure of cutting, heaping and burning the bush. Then there are innumerable references to planting (with hoes) and manuring ("carrying dung from the cow-pen") and, as the plants grew (or did not), an endless succession of thinning, "filling up the blanks," "trimming cotton," weeding (more burning), cutting suckers.

Harvesting was equally varied: "cutting Guinea Corn," "bracking (ie. breaking) Indian corn," stripping or shucking Indian Corn, thrashing Guinea Corn, "gathering (a variety of) pease," "striping fodder," gathering corn stalks, picking cotton, "diging yams". . . .

By way of diversion, there were always houses to build, to paint and

3

to repair. First, the acquisition of the building materials: cutting thatch, "getting leaves and wattles," "diging rock," burning lime, bringing sand. Next, a variety of construction work: tying on wattles, "mixing morter," "priming up the wall," thatching, ridging, building a stone gable-end, white-washing (inside and outside), "doing carpenter's work," "laying floor."

Roads also needed frequent attention: making ("clearing a track"), cleaning, repairing, "weeding public road."

Major H. MacLachlan Bell gathered the following account from an old lady who grew up on her grandfather's estate on Great Exuma (1934: 161-62):

The slaves had their quarters in palmetto huts, some owned beds of woven mats, others slept on the floors. Their wells were shallow and they scooped up their drinking supply by stooping from steps that ran down into the water. They used basins for dishes and employed broad leaves for ceremonial service when visitors appeared. These servitors received a pint of corn daily and ground it for themselves after finishing the field labor. They cooked this outside the kitchens on open fires. Three stones held their pots. After supper came rest. Often a fiddler played and the blacks danced until nine o'clock. "And then to Bed."

"These folks were simple, happy and contented," said my friend. "They got food even if the crops failed. They were allowed one pig to each family and some chickens. When these were sold they got one-third the price in cash or goods. The men wore blue denim and the women white and check cottons. . . ."

Some information concerning slave marriages may be found in a comprehensive amendment, passed in 1826, to the consolidated slave law. It specified in detail the rights and duties of the slave and his master. According to Wright, the section on marriage made the following provisions (1905: 447):

The Bahama slave code professed to encourage legitimate marriages among the slaves of the colony, and between slaves and free blacks. . . . With a view to the religious and moral improvement of the slaves, it

4

was attempted to promote the attachment of husbands and wives among them, and to prevent, as far as possible, polygamy and promiscuity of conjugal relations. . . . Registers of marriages were kept. Very primitive ideas prevailed among these poor people as to the duties conceived by Englishmen, to be assumed when entering into the marriage contract. Regulations were made for the purpose of inculcating proper ideas as to the mutual obligations of husband and wife, and urging upon them the importance of remaining together when once united. Neither husband or wife was saleable unless the other was sold at the same time, and to the same purchaser. Children were not allowed to be separated from their parents until they had reached the fourteenth age.

There is no evidence as to what degree these laws were enforced. Probably the strong missionary zeal in the islands during the first half of the nineteenth century resulted in their enforcement (Dowson 1960).

Following the Emancipation in 1838 some plantation owners gave their land to their former slaves when they left the "Cotton Islands," Lord Rolle of Exuma being the best-known example (Mosely 1926: 75). Many of these freed slaves in gratitude adopted the names of their former owners (Powles 1888: 298). I have been unable to ascertain if this was a legal transfer of land. At the time of the Emancipation the English captured a number of Spanish slave ships and set their human cargos free. Some of these Negroes went to the Exumas and Long Island and intermarried with the freed slaves, who were tilling the soil of the abandoned plantations. This increased the number of occupants on the depleted land to a point where migration became necessary, and so Long Island and the Exumas experienced a decline in population after 1861 (Sharer 1955: 85).

Tribal Origins. The Negroes the Loyalists brought with them from the American colonies had come from West Africa, while the Negroes from the captured slave ships were from the Congo. The shift of the slave trade from West Africa to the mouth of the

5

Congo River after 1800 (Herskovits 1941: 33-53) accounts for the two different origins. Tribes represented in the Bahamas at one time included Nangos, Congos, Congars or Nangobars, Ebos, Mandingos, Fullahs, Haussas, Yourabas, and Egbas (Rawson 1864: 18; Powles 1888: 147; Bell 1934: 81). The freed Congo slaves were settled in special villages on New Providence and some of the other islands, including Long Island (Wright 1905: 515-19). After 1835 Negroes who moved to the out-islands (any island in the Bahamas other than New Providence) "were usually composed of ex-slaves freshly transplanted from Africa, mixed in language and custom" (Sharer 1955: 67). Some of these Negroes settled on the Exumas; others seem to have settled at the northern end of Andros, which is only 25 miles from New Providence. Alice Northrop, a naturalist who visited Andros in 1890, reports having talked to a woman in Mastic Point "whose mother and father were full-blooded Congos" (1910a: 14).

First Settlements on Northern Andros. The earliest settlements on Andros were established in the latter half of the eighteenth century by a few white families and their Negroes, followed by a number of Loyalists and their slaves. By 1788, 88 Loyalists, 16 native Bahamians, and 254 Negroes had made northern Andros their home (Sharer 1955: 35). From 1780 to 1838 the population, which was concentrated at the northern end of the island, never numbered more than 500. The main industries were cutting timber and raising cotton (Sharer 1955: 33-34, 59-60). Profits from lumbering were short-lived because overintensive cutting destroyed the hardwood forests (Crowley 1956b; 239). Likewise, cotton production rapidly declined because of soil exhaustion (Forsyth 1930: 10). From the time of Emancipation to 1870 "most of the settlers were moving into the northern half of the island where the main centers of population were Staniard Creek, Nichols Town, and Mastic Point" (Sharer 1955: 61).

6

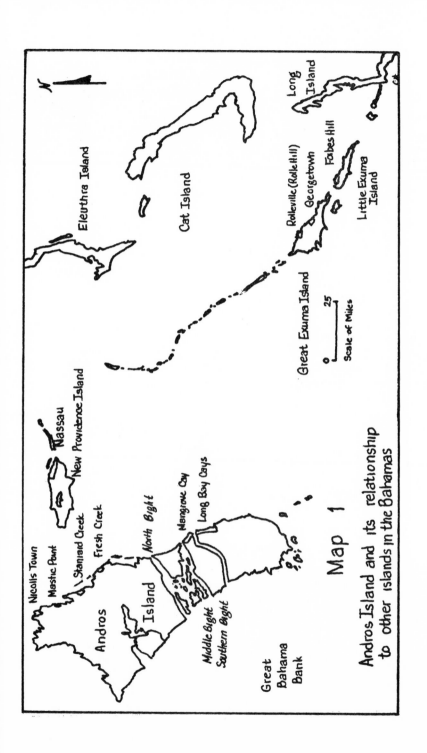

Map 1

Andros Island and its relationship
to other islands in the Bahamas

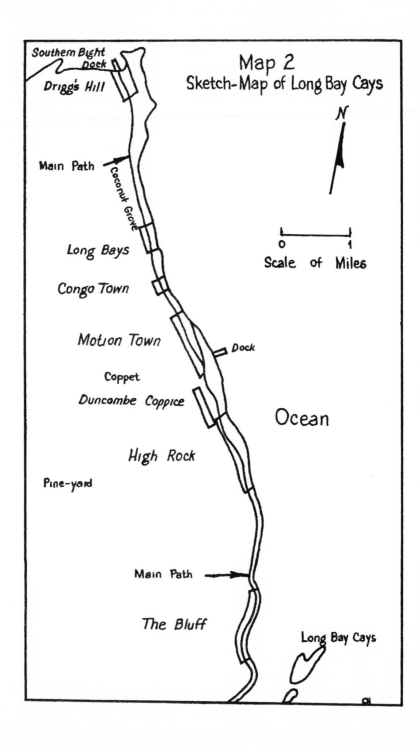

Map 2
Sketch-Map of Long Bay Cays

N

Southern Bight Dock
Drigg's Hill
Main Path
Coconut Grove
Long Bays
Congo Town

Scale of Miles
0   1

Motion Town
Dock
Coppet
Duncombe Coppice

Ocean

High Rock

Pine-yard

Main Path

The Bluff

Long Bay Cays

First Settlements on Southern Andros. Many grandparents and great-grandparents of the present inhabitants of southern Andros came from the Exumas and Long Island, 100 miles to the south-east of Andros, during the latter half of the nineteenth century in search of free land (Sharer 1955: 61). As mentioned above, the exhausted soil of these islands could not support the increase in population caused by the influx of Congo Negroes. The desire for virgin soil led the migrants to choose southern Andros, which seems to have been uninhabited, for their new home. Many of the new settlers squatted on "Crown land," neither buying nor rent-ing it from the government (Powles 1888: 80). Others bought land in ten- or twenty-acre plots from the Crown. One may con-jecture that the migration must have taken several decades: the first families to arrive probably sent word to relatives left behind that free land was available.

Many people in Long Bay Cays can trace their ancestry back to Exuma, some even being able to specify the part of the island from which their ancestors came, such as Forbes Hill and Rolle Hill. These people have the same surnames as the former owners of the plantations—Forbes and Rolle. Some who said their grandparents came from Exuma also claim to have had ancestors who were "Conga People." Conga People, reputed to have been of short stature, settled in the area now called Congo Town. (Congo was the only tribal name I was able to obtain from informants in southern Andros.)

Even though the first settlers to southern Andros were farmers interested in agriculture, the rapidly developing sponge industry in the northern half of the island attracted many of the men to this area. Not only men from southern Andros were drawn to the area, but also fishermen from many parts of the Bahamas. Ac-cording to Sharer (1955: 61-62): "Another post-Civil War de-velopment was the greatly increased activity in sponge fishing. The 'Mud' attracted boatmen from all around. Many sponging vessels accustomed to picking up their crews in Nassau soon began to lose their men to Andros where many of them married and settled down." Consequently, as indicated in Table 1, the population of Andros increased rapidly during the latter half of the nineteenth century, males exceeding females in number until after the census of 1911.

From 1865 to 1938, when the sponge beds were devastated by a marine disease, sponge fishing was the primary source of income for the Andros Islanders. The annual value of the "catch" was £60,000, about 60 per cent of which went to the fishermen (Powles 1888: 92-93). This income was high compared with their subsistence needs. Since most of the food consumed came from their own fields, they needed money only to purchase clothing and groceries such as condiments, shortening, and leavening. A description of several houses on Andros in 1890 gives no indication

TABLE 1

POPULATION OF ANDROS[a]

Year	Males	Females	Total
1851	520	510	1,030
1861	696	670	1,366
1871	n.i.	n.i.	2,138
1881	n.i.	n.i.	3,434
1891	2,312	2,277	4,589
1901	3,192	3,155	6,347
1911	3,875	3,670	7,545
1921	3,431	3,545	6,976
1931	3,577	3,494	7,071
1943	3,156	3,562	6,718
1953	3,327	3,809	7,136

n.i.=no information.

[a] Sources of data: 1851 and 1861 (Rawson 1864: 93-94); 1871 and 1881 (Government of Bahamas, *Blue Book* 1872 and 1881); 1891 to 1953 (census reports for 1901 to 1953).

that this income was used to improve living quarters (Northrop 1910a: 6, 7, 12, 14). Evidently the islanders were able to spend a large portion of their earnings on liquor.

When the fishermen returned home from a sponging trip, after having spent several weeks on the "Mud," they would go on a drunken spree for several days. Bell (1934: 149) states: "The Androsian is a fellow of parts who spends most of his time on the great sponge beds on the west coast known as The Mud. Now and again when at home he fills up on cheap rum and makes the settlement feel his presence. Then it behooves officialdom to lock him up. Sobered in time, he goes back to sea, not only with resignation but with alacrity—he has had his 'binge.'" This practice, however, had existed prior to the development of the sponge industry. According to Schoepf, who visited the Bahamas in 1784 (1911: 276): "After a profitable or heavy catch, the fishermen dispose themselves to drinking up their gains rather than to taking thought of their own needs or those of the market." Even today, intoxication is looked upon by most men as a desirable state.

Both the men and the women who migrated to southern Andros had learned to work fields during slave days (McKinnen 1804: 183), but many men became sponge fishermen because of the excellent cash return for their work. Thus "the majority of the men were engaged in sponging, and the women in consequence did most of the work in the fields" (Northrop 1910a: 24). By 1900 the economic life of southern Andros was firmly based upon agriculture, which provided the subsistence crops, and on sponging, which provided the cash needed to buy groceries, clothes, and the much sought-after rum. However, as the economy came to depend more and more on sponge fishing, agriculture was neglected (Forsyth 1929: 16; 1930: 12; 1931: 12). Many men "had come to despise work in the fields, regarding it as only fit for women and old men" (Forsyth 1930: 10).

11

The increase in fishermen resulted in an overworking of the sponge beds, and profits began to decline. "In 1917 £152,000 worth of sponge was exported from the Bahamas, but in 1923 the exports fell to £112,300" (Mosely 1926: 138). A series of hurricanes in the late twenties destroyed many of the sponge beds (Forsyth 1929: 16-17; 1930: 11; 1931: 8-11), and in 1938 the sponges virtually became extinct from a blight. Some of the sponge beds, which have recovered, were opened for three months in 1956 (*Bahamas: Report for the years 1956 and 1957*, 1959: 26).

The decline of the sponge beds resulted in a population decrease (see Table 1), caused largely by male migration. According to the 1921 census, the number of females, for the first time in the history of Andros, exceeded the number of males. As indicated in Table 2, this migration pattern also held true for southern Andros, which includes Mangrove Cay and all settlements south.

TABLE 2

POPULATION OF SOUTHERN ANDROS

Year	Males	Females	Per cent of Married Men Absent	Total
1901	1,383	1,430	....	2,813
1911	1,659	1,763		3,422
	(452)*	(485)	7	
1921	1,456	1,817		3,273
	(414)	(518)	20	
1931	1,331	1,790		3,121
	(360)	(520)	31	
1943	1,637	1,927		3,564
	(510)	(610)	16	
1953	1,573	1,960	....	3,533

* The numbers of married persons are given in parentheses. The category "married females" in the census reports does not include widows (they are enumerated in another column). All the figures above except percentages come from the census reports for the respective years.

Lack of employment on Andros, after the sponge beds were closed, forced men to travel to other islands in the Bahamas or to the United States to seek work. According to Sharer (1955: 63): "By about 1941 the war demand for agricultural workers in the United States came to the rescue of a large number of ex-fishermen who migrated there temporarily. From about 1945 on, approximately 15 per cent, never more than a thousand, of the Andros population has been steadily engaged in seasonal farm work in the States."

Sponge fishermen, as described above, would spend the greater part of the year either at sea or at the northern end of the island, leaving their wives at home. This temporary male absenteeism has been a constant feature of the economic life of southern Andros since the time of its earliest settlement. In a community where there is no temporary male absenteeism and the people are monogamous, the number of married men and women should be equal. Therefore, the number of married women minus the number of married men present at a particular time gives the exact number of married men who are temporarily absent from the community. This statement assumes that the married men have not deserted their wives. As shown in Table 2, the number of men temporarily absent divided by the number of married men who belong to the community (i.e., the same figure as the number of married women) gives the percentage of married men who are temporarily absent. Fortunately, the census reports for 1911 through 1943 include the number of married persons for southern Andros. Since the census takers record where a person is staying at the time the census is taken, and not where the person lives, the above formula can be used to calculate the degree of temporary male absenteeism for southern Andros. The number of married men is appreciably lower than the number of married women, the rate of temporary male absenteeism running as high as 31 per cent. This constitutes conclusive evidence that

13

temporary male absenteeism has been characteristic of southern Andros for many years.

In summary, the first settlers of southern Andros were farmers who brought with them from the Exumas and Long Island a fully developed agricultural tradition. The sponge fishermen, who came from other islands in the Bahamas, merged their way of life with the basically agrarian economy. This occurred through marriages between fishermen and local women and through local men adopting a maritime way of life. Becoming seamen was not only a means by which men could live a more exciting life, but also a way of obtaining a cash income to supplement the subsistence economy. With the decline of the sponge industry some Bahamians, principally men, left the island. Sponge fishing, however, produced temporary male absenteeism, for men would be at sea or in northern Andros for several months at a time. One effect of this temporary absenteeism was to place the greater burden of the agricultural work on the women. The destruction of the sponge beds did not alter the pattern of absenteeism, for new work opportunities as agricultural laborers appeared in the United States.

SETTLEMENT PATTERN

All that is visible of Long Bay Cays from a distance at sea is the blue-green ocean washing upon a narrow, sandy beach backed by rows of coconut palms. Only here and there, where a break occurs in the coconut groves, can one find an occasional house. Behind the houses is a ridge covered with a thick growth of tropical trees and shrubs known as the "bush." There are only two docks for the entire settlement district: a main dock at Motion Town built for the weekly mail boat to unload mail, passengers, and supplies, and a smaller dock at Drigg's Hill.

The seven villages which compose Long Bay Cays are connected by a path, 50 to 200 yards back from the shore line. Be-

14

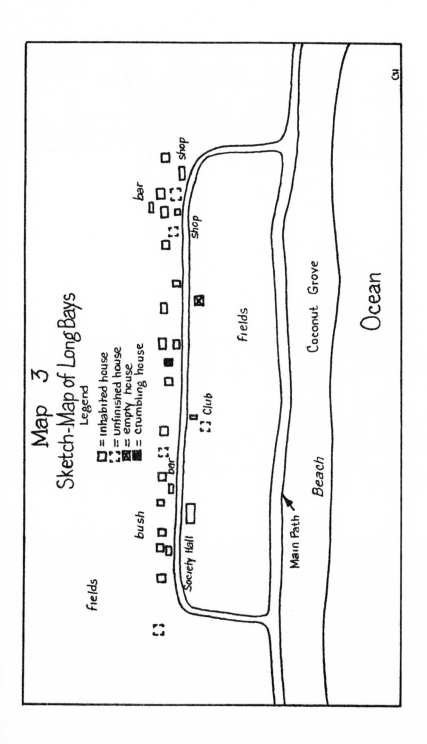

Map 3

Sketch-Map of Long Bays

Legend

□ = inhabited house
:: = unfinished house
⊠ = empty house
■ = crumbling house

fields

bush

Society Hall

bar

Club

Shop

bar

shop

fields

Main Path

Beach

Coconut Grove

Ocean

CH

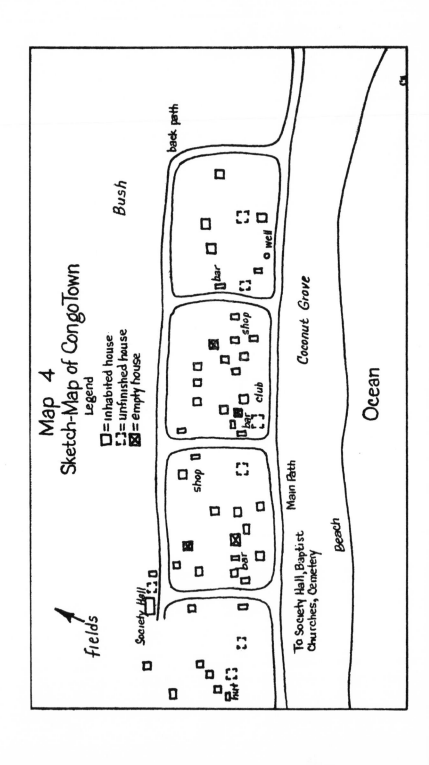

tween the path and the shore are the coconut groves. In some places the path is so narrow that it would be difficult to drive through in a car or truck. At present this is no problem to the people of Long Bay Cays, because they own no cars, only a few bicycles. Thus visiting between villages is restricted almost entirely to walking. The distance from one village to another varies from a few yards to two miles, but it is more meaningful to list distances in terms of walking time rather than mileage. From north to south the walking time between villages is as follows: Drigg's Hill to Long Bays is one hour; Long Bays to Congo Town is fifteen minutes; Congo Town to Motion Town is fifteen minutes; Motion Town to Duncombe Coppice is fifteen minutes; Duncombe Coppice to High Rock is three minutes; High Rock to The Bluff is half an hour.

The houses in each village are scattered along the main path, so that settlement patterns are lineal. Many houses are built on the side of the path away from the shore, the trees and bush providing some protection from the impact of hurricanes. Most houses have limestone walls and wooden shingle roofs. In addition to houses, the villages have bars, small grocery shops, churches, clubs (a club is a bar with a dance hall), schools, and society halls or lodges. Motion Town also has a telegraph station and a post office-courthouse. The society hall is used by a burial society—the type commonly found in New World Negro communities—for its meetings. A society's purpose is the collection of dues to provide a treasury large enough to insure a decent burial for each member and his immediate family.

The four villages in which the census was conducted contain the following nonresidential buildings: Long Bays has two bars, two shops, no churches, and one society hall (see Map 3). A club is being built. Congo Town has three bars, two shops, two Baptist churches, and two society halls (see Map 4; the churches and one of the society halls are not shown on the map, since they lie south of the village). A large, two-story club is being built in Congo Town. Motion Town has two bars, three shops, an Anglican church, one society hall, a telegraph office, a school, a post office-courthouse, and a dock (see Map 5). Children from all four villages and High Rock attend the school. The enrollment in 1959, according to the constable, was 104 boys and 79 girls. Drigg's Hill and The Bluff have their own schools. Duncombe Coppice has two bars, one shop, one club, one Church of God, and one society hall (see Map 6).

Since the people of these four villages interact frequently, they can be considered a "community" in the sense of being "the maximal group of persons who normally reside together in face-to-face association" (Murdock *et al.* 1961: 89). The community, however, has no name for itself. The four villages are spatially separated from Drigg's Hill and socially separated from High Rock. A walking distance of one hour provides an interaction barrier between Long Bays and Drigg's Hill. Between Duncombe Coppice and High Rock there is no such barrier; nevertheless, the people of Duncombe Coppice visit the three villages north of them in preference to High Rock. This visiting pattern has resulted from the failure of High Rock residents to participate in events held by Duncombe Coppice and Motion Town. Several years ago these two villages helped High Rock in a Red Cross fund-raising drive; High Rock did not help Motion Town when it later held its drive. They also disapprove of the attitude of the men in High Rock. Though they attend dances in other villages, at their own dances they will not let their wives and daughters dance with men from such villages. Consequently, people from Duncombe Coppice and Motion Town consider High Rock people to be unfriendly, and therefore visit them only when necessary.

Demography

According to a census taken by the constable-postmaster in January 1959, the population of Long Bay Cays was 1,247. A

18

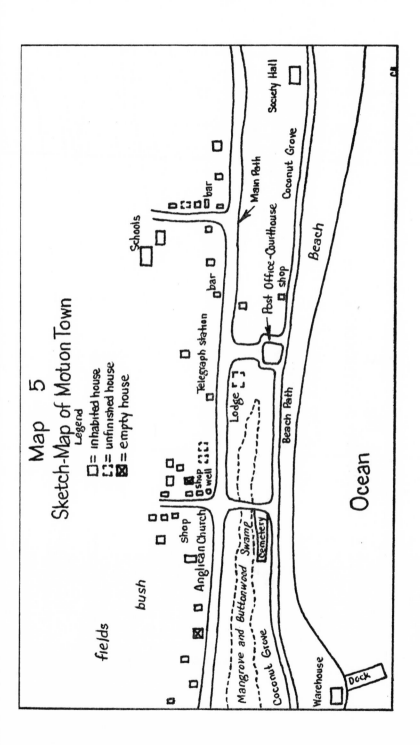

Map 5
Sketch-Map of Motion Town

Legend
☐ = inhabited house
⊡ = unfinished house
⊠ = empty house

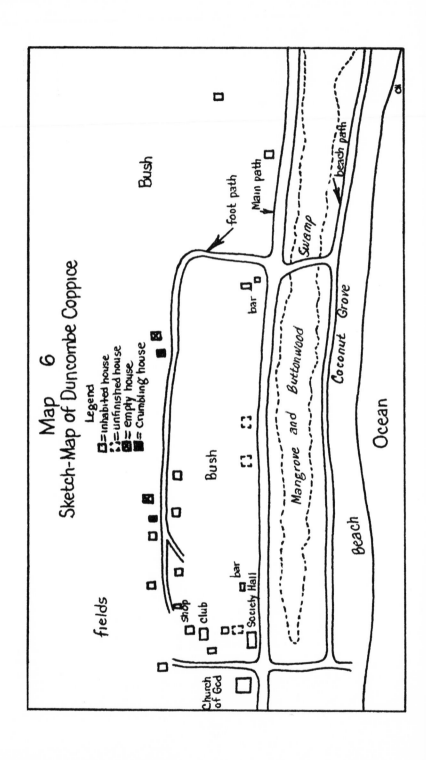

Map 6
Sketch-Map of Duncombe Coppice

Legend
☐ = inhabited house
⊡ = unfinished house
▨ = empty house
■ = crumbling house

TABLE 3

POPULATION OF LONG BAY CAYS, JANUARY 1959

Village	Number of People
Drigg's Hill	248
Long Bays	112
Congo Town	147
Motion Town	91
Duncombe Coppice	77
High Rock	235
The Bluff	337
Total	1,247

comparison of Table 3 with Table 4 shows that the population of each of the four smallest villages is higher than the figures I recorded during the summer of 1961. This discrepancy stems

TABLE 4

POPULATION AND NUMBER OF HOUSEHOLDS IN THE FOUR VILLAGES, JUNE 1961

Village	Number of People	Number of Households
Long Bays	94	16
Congo Town	129	35
Motion Town	86	22
Duncombe Coppice	47	12
Totals	356	85

from the different criteria for household membership used by the recorders. The constable enumerated people who belonged to Long Bay Cays—belonged in the sense of being born and reared there. He included in his census young adults who have left Long Bay Cays and will probably not be returning. On the other hand,

21

I recorded only those persons who were regarded by the villagers as being members of their community. If a conversation with the parents indicated that their children would not be returning, they were not enumerated. Consequently, my criteria resulted in lower census figures than the constable's totals. However, if a person was temporarily absent from Long Bay Cays even for a number of months—for instance, if a husband was away on a fishing trip— he or she was counted in my census.

Analysis of the age distribution of the population indicates that many young men and women are leaving the community (see Table 5), for the majority of the population (57 per cent) is under 21 years of age, and only 16 per cent of the population is in the age range from 21 to 40. Such migration has been characteristic of the entire island for nearly 50 years. However, the fact that there are more persons in the age range from 41 to 60 (19 per cent) than in the age range from 21 to 40 (16 per cent) may indicate that some of them are returning and making Long Bay Cays

TABLE 5

AGE AND SEX OF POPULATION

Age Group	Males	Females	Total
0 - 10	61	68	129
11 - 20	35	40	75
21 - 30	16	18	34
31 - 40	10	11	21
41 - 50	20	21	41
51 - 60	14	13	27
61 - 70	7	12	19
71 - 80	2	5	7
81 - 90	1	1	2
91 - 100	1	0	1
Totals	167	189	356

their home. Another interpretation might be that the percentage of migrants has increased.

Analysis of sex ratios indicates that both young men and women have left the community. (Sex ratio is computed by dividing the number of females by the number of males, the ratio being designated as F/M). In the age range from 21 to 60 there are only three more women than men (1.05 F/M). Many men, as described earlier, have left the area to find work, and women are also leaving to find work in Nassau. Unfortunately, our data cannot answer the question of motivation: are the women leaving merely to seek employment, or because there is a shortage of marriageable men? It would be necessary to interview these women in Nassau to be able to answer the question. However, from the point of view of a structural analysis of the community, what is important is that there is not a surplus of females in the community. In many parts of the New World where there is heavy male migration, unmarried women mate with married men, single men not being available.

There is, however, a surplus of females in the lowest and the highest age ranges. Under the age of twenty-one there are twelve more girls than boys (1.14 F/M). This probably results from both a higher male infant mortality rate and a higher rate of male migration. Over the age of sixty there are seven more women than men (1.64 F/M), the surplus resulting from the greater longevity of women.

ECONOMY

Local agriculture and offshore fishing furnish the subsistence of the inhabitants of Long Bay Cays. Local produce, however, does not provide a cash crop. Ever since southern Andros was first settled, temporary absenteeism has been necessary for most men to supplement the subsistence economy. Today, just as in the past, men must leave their homes and engage in work which

23

provides the money for purchasing clothing, groceries, and building materials. Before 1940 the money was earned by sponging; today it is earned largely through crawfishing and working as argicultural laborers in the United States. This section will describe not only the subsistence economy but also the various means by which men earn the necessary cash.

Agriculture. The fields, which are used in shifting cultivation, are often located several miles back in the "bush" on the oölitic limestone ridge which runs the length of the island. Many persons have several fields, each under an acre in size, located in different areas. Surrounding each field are uncleared areas, which may or may not have once been cultivated. When a field is abandoned, a new one is selected in the uncleared area.

Land is either individually owned or belongs to the Crown (Bahamas Government). The owned land has been inherited from ancestors who purchased the land in ten- and twenty-acre plots in the latter part of the nineteenth century. Farmers prefer to use Crown land, which is available without leasing, rather than to exhaust the scanty soil on their own land. Since Crown land is plentiful and the population is sparse (4.46 persons per square mile on Andros, according to the 1953 census), there is no competition for fields.

Many of the crops which were grown on the "Cotton Islands" are also being raised in southern Andros today. A comparison of the crops listed in Farquharson's journal with those listed in Table 6 shows Guinea corn, Indian corn, pigeon peas, cowpeas, yams, and sweet potatoes to be characteristic of the subsistence economies of both areas. However, there have been changes in the relative importance of some of the crops in the total economy. Guinea corn, the chief crop 130 years ago on Watlings Island, is now of minor importance. It has been replaced in the local diet by rice, which is purchased in Nassau. Indian corn is today the most important subsistence crop.

24

TABLE 6

PLANTING AND HARVESTING CYCLES OF CROPS

Crop	Planting	Harvesting
Indian corn (*Zea mays*)	January-March August-September	August (same year) March-April (next year)
Pigeon peas (*Cajunus cajun*)	February-April	February-April (next year)
Cassava (*Manihot esculenta*)	Any time	May remain in ground as long as 3 years
Sweet potatoes (*Ipomoeas batatas*)	Any time, March best	12 months later
Yams (*Dioscorea alata L.*)	March-April	March-April (next year)
Cowpeas (*Vigna unguiculata*)	May-June	October-December (same year)
Guinea corn (*Sorghum vulgare*)	March-May	December (same year)

Shifting cultivation, as practiced in southern Andros, is based on a slash-and-burn clearing technique. Following the selection of the uncleared area to be used for the new field, the brush is chopped down with a "cutlass" (machete), heaped into piles, and burned. The brush which does not burn is repiled and burned again. The soil is then prepared for planting by being turned over with a short-handled hoe or with a cutlass. The cutlass is a more useful implement, because it "can reach down into the pockets in the rocks" (Mooney 1905: 172). Tubers are planted by hand. A "plantin' stick" (a long pointed pole) is used in planting seeds. The farmer pokes around in the ashy earth until he finds a soft spot in which he can make a hole. After two or three grains have been dropped into the hole, it is closed with the heel of the bare foot. Once the plants start to grow, they are weeded carefully with a cutlass.

Crops are planted during the months of greatest rainfall— January through March, and August. Indian corn is the first crop of the year to be planted. Pigeon peas and cassava are planted next in the same field with the corn. The peas are planted away from the corn stalks if the farmer wants to plant a second crop of corn in August. If he plants them close to the corn, the ripening pea vines—pigeon peas take a year to ripen—will choke out the young corn sprouts which spring up in September. Harvesting occurs when the crops are ripe (grains) or when they are needed (root crops).

Some farmers are omitting the August planting because they believe the seasons are changing. I was told that rain is coming in January now rather than March. If Indian corn were planted in August, it would be ripening in January. The presence of a growing crop would prevent planting at the first of the year, when the farmers could take advantage of the rain. After the harvest in March it would be too dry to plant. Farmers, however, could switch their main planting month from January to August. Interestingly enough, January was not the main month for planting Indian corn nearly two hundred years ago. According to Schoeph, who visited the Bahamas in 1784 (1911: 269): "Maize yields but one harvest a year, the character of the seasons not admitting of two plantings. It cannot be put into the ground until the rainy season has begun, in June or July that is, and thus does not mature until November or December. . . . The dryness of the other months does not permit of a second seeding."

After the crops are harvested, the field is weeded in preparation for a second planting. A field will be used two or three times, after which it will be allowed to remain fallow for approximately six years. However, weeding may be so difficult after a harvest that it is easier to start a new field. One reason for this is that pigeon peas have long, strong roots which make the ground hard to weed. For these reasons fields are often abandoned before the soil is exhausted.

Many fruits are also grown. The most important ones in the local diet are coconuts, sugar cane, sapodillas, mangoes, limes, bananas, oranges, grapefruit, avocados, guavas, soursops, sugar apples, and plums. Though fruit trees and bushes are planted, little time is spent caring for the growing plants. One reason, perhaps, is that children steal much of the fruit before it is ripe (Otterbein 1959). Another reason is that the people consider fruit of secondary importance in their diet, and therefore eat it as snacks during the day rather than at mealtime. Of course, from a nutritional point of view fruit is an important part of the native diet.

Fishing. Fishing provides not only another basic source of food for the Andros Islanders but also a cash income. Several kinds of fishing are carried on. Since the late 1930's sponge fishing has been of no importance in the economy. However, another type of fishing, nearly as lucrative, has taken its place—crawfishing. When the season opens on the first of October, sailing vessels transport the fishermen and their dingies to the fishing grounds. The season closes the fifteenth of March. The owner of the dingy has a man scull for him while he uses a long pole to prod the crawfish out from under the rocks. When a crawfish emerges, the fisherman tosses his pole to the sculler, picks up a ring net, and drops it over the crawfish.

The earnings of each man from this type of fishing are high. The crawfish sell for £7 to £9 a hundred (the pound sterling is valued at $2.80 in the Bahamas). During a five- or six-week fishing trip a vessel may earn between £500 and £600, the owner receiving one-fourth of the earnings. The captain is either the owner or is paid out of the owner's share. The grocery bill is paid from the remaining three-fourths of the earnings. Each fisherman and each dingy receives one share of the remaining money. A vessel usually carries a crew of nine, including the captain, and four dingies. As an example of the sharing, if the crawfish sold for £560, the vessel's share would be £140. If groceries cost £36, this would leave £384 to be divided into twelve £32 shares. Since the owner of a dingy usually gives the sculler at least one-fourth of the boat's share, each fisherman will receive either £56 or £40. As in the days of sponge fishing, some of this money is used for a "binge."

Some fishermen engage in "scale-fishing" (fishing for any fish with a scaly exterior) after the crawfish season closes. These men spend approximately two weeks fishing and a third week delivering the fish to market in Nassau. A "smock-boat"—a vessel with an enclosed well for keeping the fish alive—carries the crew to the fishing area. Baited traps are taken from the vessel in dingies and dropped to the ocean bottom, each dingy carrying two or three traps. These traps are checked periodically during the day, and at night are removed from the ocean. While the fishermen are waiting for the traps to fill, they fish with hooks and lines from the vessel and boats.

The earnings from scale-fishing are low in comparison with those from crawfishing. Shares are computed in the same manner. For example, if the value of the catch is £60, the owner receives £15. If groceries cost £9 and if there are four crew members besides the captain and two dingies, each fisherman receives only £6, plus part of the dingy share. The financial return to the individual fisherman, unless he owns the vessel, is very low. If a man has to work nearly a month for £5 to £10, many, understandably, do not even bother to go scale-fishing.

Fishing close to shore with hand lines provides most of the fish which are consumed locally and which form an important part of the diet. A man will go out in the morning in his dingy and return in the mid-afternoon in order to sell the fish he has caught.

Only a few in the community do such fishing. Since most of the fish caught are small, the fisherman sells them in lots, and on a good day he can net £1. His wife or an adolescent boy may go with him to help scull. Women and children often fish from the shore, wading out into the water until it nearly reaches their waists before casting their lines. The fish thus caught are eaten by the members of the angler's household.

Though conch, grunt, loggerhead turtle, margate fish, porgy, and turbot are caught inside the reef all year round, there are shorter fishing cycles for other fish. The cycle for barracuda, hog fish, shad, and snapper is June and July; for bone fish and shark, October through February; for grouper, November through January; and for mutton fish, June through September.

Wage Labor. Farming and fishing provide the subsistence diet of the inhabitants of Long Bay Cays, but, except for crawfishing, neither of these activities provides enough money to build a house or manage a household, even if some of the produce and fish are sold. Since groceries, clothes, household furnishings, and house repairs can be obtained only through cash expenditures, men must perform wage labor.

On the other hand, little opportunity for employment is available in the community. Only the schoolteachers, the telegraph operator, and the constable-postmaster are employed full-time. One man has a part-time job looking after the warehouse at the end of the dock. Occasionally the government hires people to build and repair the local paths. For this job men are paid £1 per day; women, 16s. per day (£1=20s.). The occupations of men and women over twenty years old are listed in Table 7. (Men who spend most of the year working in other areas are not included in the table.) Although most people engage in several occupations, for the purposes of tabulation individuals have been classified by the occupation to which they devote the greater part of their time. Many men who are listed as fishermen also raise crops. All the

29

bartenders, as well as the constable-postmaster, the preacher, and the mason, work fields. Most women are both housekeepers and farmers. Older women, who have few household tasks, devote more time to farming; younger women spend most of their time caring for the home. Men who own bars are regularly assisted by their wives. It is apparent that there is little occupational variety or opportunity in the community. Men are largely farmers and fishermen; their wives, housekeepers and farmers.

Since there is little opportunity for work in the area, many men seek jobs elsewhere. They serve in the United States as agri-

TABLE 7

OCCUPATIONS OF ADULTS IN THE COMMUNITY

Occupations	Number of Participants
Male:	
Farmer	16
Fisherman	8
Bartender	7
Teacher	3
None[a]	3
Telegraph operator	1
Constable-postmaster	1
Preacher	1
Mason	1
Total	41
Female:	
Housekeeper	44
Farmer	27
None[b]	4
Bartender	1
Total	76

[a] Boys about twenty years old without jobs.
[b] Old women who do not work.

cultural laborers, in Nassau as skilled laborers, and at resort islands in the Bahamas as service personnel and domestics. Forty-two per cent (30 out of 71) of the adult male population (those over twenty years old) spends most of its time away from Andros. Six men regularly go to the United States; eighteen men work in Nassau; six men at Cat Cay, a resort island. (Three women work in Nassau; another two at Cat Cay.)

A man's first trip to the United States as an agricultural laborer is undertaken before he is twenty. This migratory labor is referred to as "going on the contract," since the arrangement for the workers is made by the Bahamas Government. Recruiters from the United States visit Andros annually and sign up the men who want to go. During the six- to nine-month period a man is gone, the government withholds a part of his wages. When the contract first began in 1943, 75 cents was withheld from the $3.00 to $5.00 earned per day by each Bahamian, to be "paid to the worker's family in the Bahamas or deposited on behalf of the worker in the Post Office Savings Bank of the Colony" (Richardson 1944: 28). Many individual workers made additional, voluntary payments above what was deducted from their wages (1944: 29). If the man is married, the money is given to his wife each month. If he is single, it is kept for him until he returns to the Bahamas, unless he stipulates that it is to be turned over to his parents.

Two-thirds of the men in the community have been "on the contract" one or more times—usually while they were young, although only six men regularly work in the United States. An analysis of the work histories of sixty men (data were not available for eleven) shows that twenty-seven men have gone "on the contract" one to four times; thirteen, five or more times; twenty, never. The one-third who have not gone are mostly older men who were middle-aged when the contract began during World War II. One of the favorite topics of conversation for men, particularly when they are in bars, is to recount their adventures in

31

the United States. Many of them have visited a large number of states, their travels sometimes taking them as far north as Minnesota.

If a man prefers not to go on the contract, he can earn a living by staying in the Bahamas, usually finding work in Nassau or at one of the resort islands. According to the *Nassau Guardian* for May 28, 1959, wage rates per hour for the jobs Bahamians engage in are as follows: waiter, 2*s*. 6*d*.; laborer, 3*s*. 6*d*.; grocery clerk, 3*s*. 6*d*.; mechanic, 9*s*.; and carpenter, 10*s*. Though a common laborer does not earn quite $4.00 a day, a recent study (First Research Corporation 1958: 30-34) shows that the real wages or purchasing power of Bahamians is two or three times that of the natives of Trinidad and Tobago, Jamaica, British Guiana, Cuba, Haiti, and Barbados. Although he earns only $4.00 a day, a man can save money because he lives with relatives in Nassau for a nominal fee while his wife and children remain in Long Bay Cays.

Main dock at Motion Town

A "smock-boat" pulled up on shore for repairs

Anglican cemetery in Motion Town

Post office-courthouse in Motion Town

Chapter II
Courtship, Marriage, and Childbirth

COURTSHIP

A YOUNG MAN of Long Bay Cays, when he is approximately eighteen years old, prepares himself for marriage by earning the money to build a house; and from the onset of puberty, a girl begins collecting household furnishings for her dowry. After having selected a potential marriage partner, a young man obtains permission from her parents to visit at their home. If after a few months of courting he and the girl want to marry, he presents an engagement ring and letter, which confirm his intentions. From the time of this official engagement until marriage, the prospective groom is permitted to be alone with his fiancée, during which time they will probably have intercourse. The house will be completed during this period.

The House. A man who grows up in Long Bay Cays learns that he must build a house for his wife; this requirement becomes a primary value to every adult male in the community. The following example illustrates the importance attached to providing a house for one's wife:

One woman was engaged for six years before marriage; during the interim she had a son by her husband-to-be. Although her fiancé was a hard worker, he drank heavily, prolonging the time required to build a house. He refused to consider living with in-laws or relatives; if she wanted to marry him, she would have to wait until the house was finished. They were married during her second pregnancy.

A young man starts saving the money to pay for building materials before he finds a girl to court. Since a house costs between £100 and £500 to build, depending upon the amount of labor supplied by the man and his relatives, the young man must leave Andros temporarily and obtain wage labor in order to earn the

33

needed money. As described in the last chapter, nearly every man, while he is in his early twenties, goes "on the contract." In fact, a young man comes to the United States as an agricultural laborer principally to earn money for a house. If a man on the contract saves only $15.00 per month for nine months, he will have accumulated $135.00 after one season. When he returns to Andros after his first trip to the United States, he will start building his house and look for a girl to court. Possibly he will both court and become engaged to a girl before returning to the United States to increase his savings. In two more seasons he will have earned enough to finish his house. While he is in the United States his family will continue construction with the funds which have been withheld from his pay by the Government.

In addition, the young man is expected to provide the major items of furniture. Many of these items, such as tables, chairs, trunks, do not entail a large expenditure, for they will come from the homes of one's parents or relatives. The only expensive piece of furniture which he may have to buy is a bed and mattress.

The Dowry. With the assistance of their mothers, girls in their teens begin accumulating linens, towels, bedspreads, and blankets. These are put away in a trunk to be used as the girl's dowry when she marries. The dowry may contain more substantial items, like a sewing machine. If a girl has no dowry, such items will be bought with the husband's money when they marry. But if they should quarrel later, the husband will not fail to list the absence of a dowry among his wife's many shortcomings.

In summary, if a man wishes to marry he must provide a house for his wife; on the other hand, the girl is expected—but not compelled—to provide a dowry. The wedding, which is described in the next section, requires no expenditure for the bride or groom, the cost being assumed by their parents.

Selection of Mates. A man is not permitted to court, or mate with, any female member of his kindred, which extends bilaterally as far as genealogical connections can be remembered by his oldest relatives. Therefore, his kindred includes all known consanguineal relatives, who are referred to by the community as being "family to him." Thus cousin marriage of any degree is prohibited. Since a kindred may have several hundred members, possibly some relatives will be unknown to the man. If he selects for a prospective wife a girl distantly related to him, his mother informs him of the relationship. Since he has not begun courting the girl, it is unlikely that there has been time for an attachment to form, so that the young man will not be disappointed and attempt to disregard the wishes of his parents.

Marriage between kin is condemned because "it is wrong." Apparently there is no thought that such a union might result in the birth of defective children, nor is there a fear of punishment by eternal damnation. There are only three known cousin marriages in Long Bay Cays. One couple did not learn they were distantly related until after their wedding. Since they did not intentionally violate community standards, they were not condemned. Another couple, who are first cousins, married despite strong opposition from the woman's mother; since the daughter was more than twenty-one, her mother could not legally prevent their marriage. The man was a widower in his forties. They avoid the pressure of community sanctions by living in Nassau. Even several years after the wedding, the woman's mother was embarrassed and ashamed when she told me about her daughter's marriage. I was unable to get data on the third couple, who were also first cousins.

Being related to many of his fellow villagers often forces a man to seek his wife in another village; three-fourths of the ninety-four marriages tabulated in Table 8 are in this category. Nearly one-fifth of them have chosen their wives from one of the other three villages which form the community.

Prelude to Courtship. Several decades ago a young man had little opportunity to meet girls, since the latter were not permitted

TABLE 8

RESIDENCE PATTERN

Form of Residence		Per cent
Village endogamy (both husband and wife grew up and are living in same village:		25
Community endogamy (both grew up in one of the four villages in the community):		
Virilocal (live in his village)	14	
Uxorilocal (live in her village)	4	
		18
Community exogamy (either husband or wife came from outside the community):		
Virilocal (wife from outside)	27	
Uxorilocal (husband from outside)	28	
		55
Neolocal (both from outside):		2
Total		100

to attend school but were kept at home under the close surveillance of their parents. Today the pattern has changed, most girls attending school. Since children from several villages—Long Bays, Congo Town, Motion Town, Duncombe Coppice, and High Rock—go to the same school, a young man is likely to meet his future wife there. In addition, young men also meet girls when they visit other villages, attend dances, travel on the mail boat, or stay in Nassau.

When a young man decides he would like to court one girl in particular, he consults his parents in order to discover their views about her family. Although people in Long Bay Cays are from the same socio-economic stratum of the society, certain "families" (groups of closely related relatives) are considered not respectable, largely because of the behavior of their women. If a girl's close female relatives have illegitimate children, the supposition is that she may be having love affairs herself and hence is undesirable as a fiancée.

In the "old days"—about three generations ago—young men often had their parents find wives for them, partly because of the difficulty of meeting suitable girls. Although most men select their own spouses, arranged marriages occasionally still occur. One young man, while on the contract, wrote to his mother and asked her to find a girl he could court when he returned. His mother then inquired of women with eligible daughters whether they would consider her son as a suitor.

Initiation of Courtship. When a young man, with the help of his parents, decides what girl he would like to court, he can send a letter to the girl's parents requesting permission to visit their home as a suitor. If the letter is not returned, he knows his request has been granted. Or as an alternative, a close relative of the man, usually a parent, may visit the girl's parents to obtain permission directly. If he is acceptable, he begins visiting their home in the afternoons, after accompanying the girl home from school or church. It is said that in the "old days" the man talked only with the girl's parents, who sat between him and their daughter. Or the girl might be in another room, in which situation he might try to gain her attention by rolling small stones across the floor toward her. Today, however, the parents go into another room of the house and let the couple talk alone. The patterns are not always followed:

Alfred, a man of twenty-three, who courted a girl of seventeen for two years, went personally to her family to get permission. When he visited the girl her relatives remained in the other rooms of the house. They are now married and settled in the new house he built for her.

Mrs. Burrows, who has a seventeen-year-old daughter, would not have approved of his conduct. If a man wishes to court her daughter, she

37

does not want him to "come with dry eyes," i.e., she would consider him unmannerly to come alone to ask for her daughter. He should send a letter or he may send his parents, but she would not be offended if he accompanied them.

Courtship can be initiated not only by the man and his family, but also by the girl and her mother. A girl without a father probably has no one to finance a large wedding for her, and, furthermore, her reputation may be in question, for she is less likely to have led a sheltered life. In order for her to obtain a suitor the following method may be resorted to. A mother who notices a man walking with her daughter may try to precipitate a courtship by inviting him to visit the house. If he accepts, the mother will ask him on the third or fourth visit—or even the second if she is eager for her daughter to marry—why he has come to the house, saying, "Is there something you want here?" If he replies, "I am in love with your daughter," she will say, "I would like to see your mother." When the young man's mother comes to the house, the girl's mother asks her daughter, in the visitor's presence, whether she wants to marry the young man. Since the mother and daughter have undoubtedly planned together for the meeting, the answer, of course, is yes.

During this stage of courtship the man continues to visit the girl's home, but if he wishes to take her to a dance, to a wake, or to any event, they must be chaperoned by her mother or another relative of the girl. After several months, if he is still acceptable as a son-in-law, he sends an official engagement letter and ring to the girl and her mother. Following the engagement the man can take his fiancée out alone.

The following case illustrates the extent to which one man violated the patterns in order to obtain the girl he loved.

Stephen met his future wife, Ellen, at a dance held at the school in Motion Town. Her aunt had brought her all the way from Drigg's

Hill. It was love at first sight. He asked her to dance. She would not. He asked if she wanted some candy. No. But he bought some and gave it to another girl to give to her. She took it. He was nineteen and she was twelve at the time. He soon began to visit her at her home and help her with school work; he told her parents, but not her, why he was coming there. Her father said she was too young to be courted; however, he was given permission to court their older daughter. He agreed so that he could continue visiting, and when his future wife walked through the room, he talked to her. Both Ellen's mother and her sister, whom he was supposed to be courting, knew what his real intentions were. In order to get the mother's support, he had to agree to wait three years before becoming engaged. Furthermore, in order not to take Ellen's mind off school work and put it on marriage, the mother did not inform her of the plan. When she was fifteen, he sent the engagement letter and ring, and they were married the following year.

The Engagement Letter and Ring. Several months after the man has begun to court the girl, he gives an engagement letter to her and her mother. The letter is important because it is the only evidence acceptable in the courts of the man's intention to marry. *The Statute Law of the Bahama Islands* (p. 1159) states that "in actions for breach of promise of marriage no plaintiff shall recover a verdict unless his or her testimony shall be corroborated by some material evidence in support of such promise." The mother insists on such a letter so that the man cannot break the engagement without provoking a lawsuit. The letter is drawn up by a lawyer, a minister, a teacher, a justice of the peace, or the commissioner for the area. The official gives a signed copy of the letter to the man and retains one himself. When the fancy package containing the engagement ring and letter is opened, the girl usually grabs for the ring and the mother for the letter. The ring, which is bought in Nassau for 28s., is a gold band with a heart on it; engagement rings are all alike.

The following is a copy of an engagement letter composed by

39

a justice of the peace for a prospective bridegroom. The letter, which cost 10*s.*, was typed entirely in capitals.

L B C
    AN IS, BA
       10TH. SEPT.———1949
MISS [girl's name],
    L B C, ANDROS ISLD.
      BAHAMAS
DEAR MISS [girl's name]:—
    I TRUST THAT THIS LETTER WILL NOT BE ALTO-GETHER A SURPRISE TO YOU, AS YOU DO KNOW TO SOME EXTENT HOW VERY DEARLY I LOVE YOU. . . . [ellipsis in original] I CANNOT REALLY EXPRESS IT IN WORDS.

    LIFE TO ME IS NOT REALLY WORTHWHILE WITH-OUT YOU. . . . [ellipsis in original] I MEAN THAT UNLESS YOU CONSENT TO BECOME MY PARTNER AND COM-PANION, THERE CAN BE NO HAPPINESS IN MY LIFE WHATEVER. I REALLY BELIEVE THAT YOU LOVE ME, AND I WISH THAT I COULD EXPRESS MY LOVE FULLY TO YOU, BUT EVEN PEN CANNOT DO THIS. HOWEVER, SUFFICE IT TO SAY, THAT I SHALL DO EVERYTHING WHICH IS POSSIBLE TO MAKE YOU HAPPY IN LIFE, AND SHALL BY THE HELP OF ALMIGHTY GOD IN THE NEAR FUTURE, MAKE YOU MY WIFE AND TRUE COMPANION. I AM HEREBY ENCLOSING OUR ENGAGEMENT RING WHICH I TRUST YOU WILL LOVE AND APPRECIATE, AND ALSO ACCEPT.

                    I REMAIN
                    GRACIOUSLY YOURS,
                    [young man's name]
PER—[signature of justice of the peace]

Termination of Engagements. If the mother decides against the proposed marriage, she merely returns the suitor's letter. A girl over twenty-one need not have her parents' permission to marry (*The Statute Law:* 1363), but most daughters comply with their parents' wishes, although a first-cousin marriage has been described in which this did not occur. If the girl wants to break the engagement and her mother will not send the letter back, she will try to find and destroy it, and thus the man cannot be legally held to the engagement by her mother. She will then ask the man to break the engagement. If he is reluctant to do this, she can quickly change his mind by having an affair with someone else.

If the man wants to break the engagement but the girl's mother refuses to return the letter, his only alternative is to prolong the engagement, during which time he will seldom visit the girl. He will also stop construction of the house. If the girl's mother files a suit against him he can claim that he is delaying only because his home is not finished. In fact, he will probably sign up for "the contract" again, for leaving Andros protects him from being held legally responsible for any child his fiancée might have by another man (*The Statute Law:* 813-16). If the man has been away from Andros for nearly a year, the magistrate will recognize that he could not be the father.

Actually, if the man keeps prolonging the engagement, the parents are likely to terminate it, knowing that even if he built a home and married their daughter he would leave her and refuse to support her or any children she might have unless legal sanctions were brought against him. Thus it is better for them to return the letter and hope that another man will court and marry her. The longer they delay, the more likely she is to become pregnant by another man, and if she should have an illegitimate child, she becomes "second-rate" and may never get married.

Virginity Valued. A man wants his fiancée to be a "maid" (virgin). One reason is the disgrace felt if he realizes that other men know his wife had affairs before she married. One man said that "if you don't get a maid, you never know when a man is standing behind a tree laughing to himself because he had her first." Another reason is the belief that if the girl has had intercourse, she will compare her fiancé with her former lover, and if he is not as proficient she will probably either break the engagement or be unfaithful later.

Today, in Long Bay Cays a man will have intercourse with his fiancée in order to learn if she is a maid, and if not he probably will try to break the engagement. Apparently the man determines the girl's virginity, not by a physical inspection, but by the way she responds to him while he is seducing her. He may also look for blood afterwards. He will also continue to have intercourse with her during the remainder of the engagement period, although he realizes that this may lead to pregnancy. If the man reports to the girl's parents that she is not a virgin, they may react either by beating the girl or by accusing him of lying.

Although virginity is highly valued, not all men will break off an engagement if they find the girl is not a maid. Actually, what a man wants is a girl who has not been promiscuous. If he has reason to believe that, although she is not a virgin, she has had intercourse only a few times with perhaps one other man, he may very well go through with the marriage, for she will probably make a good wife who will stay at home and be faithful, which is what he really wants.

Although every adult in the community knows that men have intercourse with their fiancées, the fiction is maintained that a girl is a virgin when she marries. This is accomplished as follows. After the wedding the husband and wife are left alone in a house. (Since they are married in the girl's village and the man's house is probably in his village, they may not be able to spend the first night in his house.) Since it is believed that a virgin experiences pain, bleeding, and difficulty in walking after the first time she has intercourse, no one expects the wife to leave the house before morning unless she was not a maid; and knowing this, she does

42

not leave it. This custom allows the villagers to conclude that she was a maid. Such a social fiction permits people to maintain their values even though they are aware that in actual practice these values are violated.

Premarital Pregnancy. It is considered a disgrace for an unwed girl to become pregnant. Not only do people make derogatory comments, but the girl's "fall" is formally recognized in the seating arrangements in church. Normally, girls sit at the front of the congregation and form a choir. If an unmarried girl becomes pregnant, this will be brought to the attention of the minister by the female leaders of the church. He "renounces" (minister's term) her behavior in a sermon and sends her to sit at the very back of the church. She must remain there until three months after she has had her child, at which time he will publicly call her back to the front of the congregation. (Married women who are pregnant remain seated in the middle of the congregation.) Furthermore, when a pregnant girl marries in the Anglican Church she must stand on the lower three steps before the altar, rather than on the upper three steps, which are reserved for girls who appear not to be pregnant.

Since it is a disgrace for a single girl to become pregnant, attempts are made to hasten the wedding of an engaged girl so that people will not learn of her condition. The effectiveness of such sanctions, however, can be questioned. I was able to ascertain the legitimacy of the first child born to twenty-eight couples, and found that seven were born prior to marriage of the parents. In one instance, a woman had a second child before marrying the father. I did not ascertain how many of these seven couples may have been engaged before their first child was born. The reason these sanctions are not effective seems to be that the value placed on building a house for one's wife takes precedence over the value of not being noticeably pregnant or having a child before marriage.

43

In fact, since people believe that premarital pregnancy hastens marriage, intercourse is tacitly encouraged by the girl's parents during the engagement period. My informants, who had not computed the number of women who had children by their husbands prior to marriage, had no grounds for rejecting this belief. This result is accomplished, as already mentioned, by permitting the couples to go out unchaperoned. The girl's parents realize that at such times they may not come directly home but slip into the bush or down to the beach, if it is night, and have intercourse. No attempts are made to prevent this from happening. Even if the pair are discovered copulating, no comment is made to them about their behavior.

Ages at First Marriage. Altogether a courtship and engagement is likely to last about three years, unless circumstances arise which hasten or delay the marriage. At the time of marriage, the girl is usually at least 16 years old and the man 23 years old. Although ideally the ages should range from 16 to 19 for the girl and from 23 to 26 for the man, the actual ages range from 15 to 26 for girls and from 20 to 31 for men, the difference in mean ages being over 4 years (see Table 9). Most girls marry at the age of 20 or 22, most men at 23. The age gap between husband and wife ranges from 0 to 13 years, the mean being 4 years (see Table 10). The most frequently occurring age gaps are 2, 3, and 4 years. These deviations from the ideal patterns probably result because many girls have difficulty in immediately finding a husband and a few marry before their house is completed, with the result that girls marry later and men marry earlier than they ideally should.

MARRIAGE

Marriage Customs. It is the responsibility of the girl's parents to pay for all the wedding expenses with the exception of the bride's dress, which is purchased by the groom's father and may cost as much as £40. He also sponsors a party the Sunday follow-

44

ing the wedding, the cost of this being nominal in comparison with that of the wedding reception. If all the preparations, parties, and dances described are carried out, the expenses to the boy's parents will be about £50 and to the girl's about £60. The families discuss wedding preparations together, and if they decide to have a big wedding, the groom's father will purchase an expensive dress for the bride, while her father will plan a large wedding and reception. Most parents spend the sums necessary to provide for all the festivities, since people in Long Bay Cays expect large weddings; however, costs can be minimized if some of the elaborate preparations are omitted. If any of the parents—particularly the fathers—of the bride and groom are dead, the wedding will undoubtedly be small, since there would be little money available for these expenditures. Presents are seldom given, and it is impossible to compensate for the costs of a wedding by inviting a large number of guests who might be expected to bring gifts.

TABLE 9

AGES AT MARRIAGE

	Men	Women
Range	20-31	15-26
Mean	24.0	19.7
Mode	23	20, 22
Total cases	(37)	(41)

TABLE 10

AGE DIFFERENCES BETWEEN HUSBAND AND WIFE

Range	Wife 2 years older
	Husband 13 years older
Mean	4 years
Mode	2, 3, and 4 years
Total cases	(36)

The amount spent depends not only upon social pressure and the financial capacity of the parents but also upon other variables such as the status of the girl. A man is more likely to have a big wedding for an only daughter or his last daughter. On the other hand, if the girl is past the ideal age for marriage, has a child, or is known to have had affairs, the wedding is likely to be a modest one. If the girl has a child (the next section shows that childbearing is a mark of adulthood), it is unnecessary to emphasize her change of status from adolescence to adulthood with a large wedding, for she has already made the transition. On the other hand, if the girl is young and has not had a child, particularly if she is believed to be a virgin, the wedding is likely to be large. In this case, the ceremonies in effect say, "Here is a girl who people may not yet believe is an adult; in order that they will realize she is one, it is necessary to indicate her change of status with elaborate festivities."

A Nassau wedding is less expensive than an out-island wedding because social convention permits a small reception. However, if the couple have many friends from the well-to-do class, they may consider it advantageous to have a large Nassau wedding because the presents received more than compensate for the expenses. Even if the couple marry in Nassau, the parents of the bride and groom may hold a party and a dance on Andros.

Several weeks before the date set for the wedding, the girl's parents notify their minister of their daughter's forthcoming marriage. The minister must be registered as a "marriage officer" (*The Statute Law:* 1356). If he is not, a minister who is registered will perform the duties. The minister records the information in "The Marriage Banns Book" and posts notification of the wedding on the door of his church "for a period extending over three Sundays" (*The Statute Law:* 1362). The "publish," as this document is called, is also read in church for three Sundays. If there is no objection, the minister grants "a certificate of the due publication of banns, in this Act referred to as the marriage officer's certificate . . ." (*The Statue Law:* 1362).

According to Bahamian law, if a person is under the age of twenty-one he or she must obtain the consent of others (*The Statute Law:* 1363). No minimal ages are set by law. Most of the residents of Long Bay Cays do not know this; they believe that the boy must be twenty-one and the girl eighteen to marry even with parental approval. This belief, of course, results in the frequent falsification of ages on marriage certificates.

On the Friday preceding the last Sunday on which the "publish" is read in church, the "bride is put away"; i.e., she moves into the house of a nearby relative and remains there until the wedding on the following Wednesday morning. She may be visited by close relatives, including the groom's. The purpose of this custom is to prevent the bride from being seen by the groom when he goes to his future in-laws' house to inquire about the wedding plans. Her parents want her to be "looking strange" (i.e., to appear more radiant and beautiful in her finery than people had expected) to the groom and to the wedding guests when she comes out of the house on the wedding day. Wednesday is the customary day for weddings. Friday and Saturday are avoided because they are "bad luck days"; if a couple marries on Saturday, it is believed that the husband will beat the wife.

On the Monday and Tuesday nights preceding the wedding, the bride's father sponsors two dances, which are usually held in a society hall rather than in his home, where preparations are being made for the wedding feast on Wednesday afternoon. The father of the bride provides rum for the musicians but nothing for the dancers. The groom may attend these dances.

On Wednesday morning the bride-to-be returns to her home and dresses in a white wedding gown. She carries either a spray of white flowers, a fan, or a prayer book. The bridesmaids wear short white gloves and similar dresses, which may be of different colors, costing approximately £8. The groom wears a black tuxedo and black bow tie; the groomsmen, black trousers, white jackets, and black bow ties.

At most weddings the roles of "father-giver" and "best man" are incorporated in the same person, usually the groom's best friend. If both a father-giver and a best man are in attendance, the girl's father is likely to serve as father-giver. The presence of both a father-giver and a best man gives prestige to the wedding.

Shortly before 10:00 A.M. the bridal procession leaves the house. The groom, meanwhile, waits in the church by himself, unless there is both a father-giver and a best man, in which case the best man stays in the church with the groom. The bridal procession passes under a decorated palm arch spanning the entrance to the girl's parents' property. The members of the procession march in the following order: The bridesmaids and groomsmen, of which there can be any number, walk arm in arm. They are followed by the maid of honor, who walks alone. The flower girls and the page walk hand in hand. Usually there are two flower girls; there may be as many as four. The bride comes next, escorted by the father-giver. The dressmaker or a child carries the train of the bride's gown. The parents do not march in the procession unless the bride's father is giving her away.

The procession enters the church, and the members take their positions facing either the altar or the congregation. In correct order, facing the altar from left to right, are the bridesmaids, the maid of honor, the bride with the father-giver behind her, the groom, the best man, and the groomsmen. The minister faces the bride and groom. The singing of hymns precedes the marriage ceremony, which begins with the reading of the section of *The Book of Common Prayer* known as "the Matrimony." Then the minister picks up the wedding ring from the cushion held by the page, blesses it, and hands it to the groom. The maid of honor takes off the bride's glove. The groom places the ring on the tip

The procession leaving the church after a wedding

Anglican church in Motion Town

Limestone house with unfinished walls

Limestone house with the walls plastered over with cement

of the middle finger of the bride's left hand and continues holding it while the minister pushes the ring all the way to the base of the finger. As the ring passes each of her finger joints, the minister recites, "In the name of the Father, the Son, and the Holy Ghost." After a prayer is read, the couple are pronounced man and wife, and the maid of honor lifts the bridal veil back over the crown or wreath so that the groom can kiss his bride. The minister then lectures the couple on the rights, duties, and responsibilities of being husband and wife. "Immediately after the solemnization of a marriage the marriage officer . . ." registers it in a book and on a form sent to the Registrar General. The bride and groom both receive a copy (*The Statute Law:* 1367). While the procession leaves by the same door it entered or a side door, the congregation rises and sings a hymn.

The bridal veil rather than the white dress is the symbol of virginity. If the woman has a child or has been pregnant, the veil is worn on the back of the head and does not cover the face. If she has been married, she wears a short white dress and a hat with a veil on the back instead of a crown or wreath.

Following the wedding the bridal party and the invited guests go to the bride's parents' home for refreshments. One group of people at a time sits down at the table to be served pound cake, soda, and wine. There may also be a table outside under a pavilion. A meal of peas and rice, fried chicken, and pork is served to the guests who have come from a long distance.

Invitations to the wedding and reception may be printed or handwritten. Since such an invitation requires a present, only persons who can afford to give one—for instance, the schoolteacher—receive invitations. If the girl or a close relative invites someone without bothering to send an invitation, a present is not required. A person who has received either an oral or written invitation is served refreshments. If refreshments are left over, people who have attended the wedding and stayed for the dance in the afternoon may be invited in and served.

Following the serving of refreshments, the bride will "cross the floor" by dancing a waltz, a quadrille, and a round dance with the groom. Since the quadrille requires two couples, the best man and the maid of honor accompany them on the dance floor. If any of them cannot dance the quadrille, it is omitted from the sequence. Shortly before the dance is over, a woman—preferably the mother of the bride—interrupts the round dance and escorts the bride into the next room. Even though there is no semblance of a struggle, this custom is called "stealing the bride off the floor." The bridesmaids and their partners then move out on the floor to dance. The bridal couple sit on the bed in the next room and listen to sermons on how to live, delivered by older people who are supposed to know. The talks usually last from five to ten minutes each, but if a speaker becomes excited the sermon may be much longer. These exhortations may take several hours, during which time the couple listen and say nothing. When they are over, the couple leave and go to their own home. They stay indoors and are brought meals by the husband's relatives until the following Sunday morning.

After the bride and groom have departed, the dance either continues in the main room of the house or is transferred to a society hall or schoolhouse. It lasts throughout the afternoon and into the early morning hours. The bride's father provides rum for the musicians.

The "turning out," which takes place in the groom's church the following Sunday morning, consists of a special service directed toward the bride and groom. The bride wears a pink dress which costs her father about £15. Several preachers, deacons, and sextons advise them on the sacredness of marriage and the rights and duties of husband and wife as described in the Bible. After church the groom's parents hold a party at their home—not a dance, since it is Sunday; the usual refreshments, including wine and rum, are served. The parents sponsor a dance on Monday night, held usually in a schoolhouse or society hall. The bride, while dancing, wears her wedding dress, which will not be worn again unless completely remade so as to be unrecognizable.

A Wedding. The most elaborate wedding I attended in Long Bay Cays (I witnessed two other weddings during the summer of 1959) varied from some of the patterns just described. The man and girl, who had been engaged for eighteen months, lived in separate villages, High Rock and The Bluff. They belonged to the Zion Baptist Church, opposite the girl's home in High Rock. The man built his house next to his father's home. The bride's mother told me that the man was twenty-two and the girl, her oldest daughter, eighteen; however, a relative of the couple told me that he was eighteen and she seventeen. It is reasonable to believe that, being a stranger, I was at first told the "official" ages. The groom's father got the "publish" four weeks before the wedding from a minister in a village ten miles away, the fee being £2 for the license and for performing the ceremony. At the time he was visiting the minister, the father hired a man to make pound cake for £3. The "publish" was posted on the door of the minister's church, and a copy was read in the Baptist Church for three Sundays. On the Friday before the wedding, the bride was "put away" in her grandmother's house, near her parents' home.

The dance on Monday night was held in the society hall. Although it was to start at 7:30 p.m. it did not get under way until a woman with her sister and daughter showed up at 8:45. At no time during the night were there more than eight women at the dance. No one seemed to be there from the groom's village. The band consisted of the traditional goatskin drum, guitar, and saw, and the bride's father provided the musicians with rum. The dance appeared to be breaking up at 12:00 p.m. but continued until 12:45 a.m. More girls attended the Tuesday night dance,

51

some even coming from a distant village. It lasted from about 9:00 P.M. until perhaps 1:00 A.M.

On Tuesday the bride's father brought the minister and the cakes to High Rock in his sailboat, and the minister stayed overnight at the girl's house. Although the wedding was scheduled for 10:00 A.M. the following morning, the minister said that by law a ceremony could only be held from 6:00 A.M. to 10:00 A.M. or from 2:00 P.M. to 8:00 P.M., which meant scheduling the wedding a half hour earlier. Since I know of no law that specifies the times for weddings, the minister may possibly have been trying to impress people with his importance. A shotgun was fired at 9:15 A.M. by one of the village men as a signal that the wedding was to begin. In fifteen minutes the church was filled with people, although some people waited in front of the house to watch the bridal procession appear, at which time another shot was fired. The four bridesmaids and two flower girls wore pink dresses. The bride, carrying a white prayer book, wore a crown rather than a wreath, and the train of her dress was carried by the seamstress. The father-giver was a good friend of the groom. The bride's father, who was dressed in old clothes, did not attend the wedding ceremony but stayed at the house preparing for the reception. The procession passed under the palm arch, around the church, and through the front door. Singing began as the procession entered the church. The minister told the congregation why the wedding could not be held at 10:00 A.M., and then he arrogantly advised the three preachers attending to observe how he performed the ceremony. When one preacher started a hymn, which was taken up by the choir, the bridal party turned and faced the congregation. The minister placed them in the following positions from left to right facing the congregation: father-giver, maid of honor, bride, groom, page, and flower girls. The minister, who stood before the bride, said that the maid of honor can provide support because she is standing beside the bride; since the groom does not need help, the father-giver does not stand next to him. The minister read the Matrimony from *The Book of Common Prayer*, and married the couple at 9:55 A.M. He then read a prayer, followed by a fifteen-minute talk on how the couple should live—faithfulness being its major theme. Since it is the wife who breaks up marriages, she should ignore any stories that her husband has a lover, and furthermore it is her responsibility to cook plenty of good food so that he does not stop at other women's houses for tea. As an illustration, he said he would not use the traditional example of Isaac and Rebekah, but that of his wife and himself. His wife had had eight children since they were married. He is not sure they are all his own; but since his wife gave them to him, he is happy he got something for nothing. Since his talk was partly humorous, muffled laughter occasionally came from the congregation; in contrast to what is usual, one heard few amens. Another hymn was "raised" as the procession left the church by the side door, stopping on the steps while people took pictures. More shots were fired, signaling the end of the ceremony.

Until 12:30 P.M. people crowded into the house and under the pavilion to eat. Peas and rice, pork, pound cake, wine, beer, rum, and soda were served. After the meal the musicians went inside the front room and played while a few couples danced. At about 1:00 P.M. the outside of the house was surrounded with people looking through the windows trying to watch the bride "cross the floor." Since the groom could not do the quadrille, only two dances were performed. The maid of honor and best man accompanied the bride and groom. The bride's mother was self-conscious about being several months pregnant, and therefore did not "steal the bride off the floor." Since I was unable to observe the dancing, I do not know who, if anyone, took the bride into the next room. In fact, the mother remained out of sight as much as possible, not even dressing up or attending the wedding ceremony. After the crossing of the floor all the guests immediately

left for the big dance at the society hall, except for a few intoxicated persons who remained behind to advise the couple on how
to live. Sometime after the couple had gone to their new home
that afternoon, the girl's mother visited her daughter. When she
left, the daughter cried; it was the first time she had been away
from her mother.

Everyone was trying to find room to dance in the crowded society hall; children were chased off the floor by adults. Some of
the men who were drunk were arguing vehemently as to who
should play the instruments and who should dance. When a fight
started at 3:15 P.M., nearly breaking up the dance, all the girls and
women immediately left the area. Some of the girls came back
after the fight had been stopped by relatives of the men, but the
life had gone from the dance, which began to break up at 6:00
P.M. but continued until 7:15 P.M.

Even though the groom's father told me that there would not
be a dance at The Bluff until Monday, some of the boy's relatives
started one in the front room of the groom's father's house before
the main dance at High Rock ended. Someone said there would
be a dance the following morning at The Bluff. By the time I got
there Thursday afternoon, a small dance was going on in the front
room of the groom's father's house. Only three or four women
were there, and most of the men were intoxicated.

The bride "turned out" at the Zion Baptist Church the following Sunday morning, the service beginning as usual at 11:30 A.M.
The couple, the bridesmaids, and the groomsmen came in the side
door because the front entrance was surrounded with rainwater.
The bride wore a pink dress, which cost the bride's father £16;
the veil was on top of her hat. Her parents fulfilled their usual
roles in church—he as the secretary and she as a member of the
choir—while the groom's parents remained at home making
preparations for the party. The minister gave a long sermon on
the moral and physical weaknesses of women, thus emphasizing

how the wife should act and be treated. In contrast, the deacon's short talk emphasized the husband's role. (The addresses which follow a sermon are referred to as "throwing light on the sermon.") Still another talk was given by the sexton, who attempted to show that the marital bond should take precedence over all other ties of kinship. He asked rhetorically, "If a wife were waiting on her husband and her mother called her, who should she serve?" A number of women responded, "Her mother." He repeated this several times and got the same reply, causing much laughter by both men and women. The bridal procession left the church after the congregation.

The guests who had been invited to the "turning-out" party walked to The Bluff immediately following the service. The party was held in the front room of the groom's father's house, people being served in shifts at a small table which could seat eight persons. The bridal procession was served first, followed by the women, the men, and finally the girls; boys were left out. Cake and beer were served. Some guests took their cake with them. After the refreshments the men continued to drink, while several of the boys and girls danced on the porch to the music of a battery-operated phonograph. The bride, who had changed to an ordinary dress, talked with the guests. They began to leave the party about 4:00 P.M. The next evening a dance, which I did not attend, was held at The Bluff in the schoolhouse.

In conclusion, I shall review what appear to be the functions of a wedding ceremony in Long Bay Cays. First, it is a rite of passage for the bride and groom; in the words of R. T. Smith (1956: 168), "It marks the passage of a couple into a legally and religiously sanctioned union, which is in conformity with the ideal values of the whole society." At the same time it communicates to kin and villagers that the bride and groom now have a new status in the community, that of married adults. Furthermore, the marriage establishes new kinship relations between some of the villagers and portends the creation of relationships that will result from the birth of children.

Second, the wedding, the reception, and the "turning out" provide ample opportunity for people to express verbally what they believe to be appropriate behavior between husband and wife. The sermons and the speeches definitely restate and confirm the ideal patterns that should govern marital relations. From this point of view the wedding serves as a rite of intensification for the community.

Third, by having a large wedding the fathers of the bride and groom can validate their claims to be important villagers. Some men in the community frequently assert their importance by voicing their opinions, by buying drinks for others, and by claiming affluence. A big wedding permits them to make good their claims and provides the opportunity for future bragging.

CHILDBIRTH

Pregnancy. Manhood and womanhood are established in Long Bay Cays by having a child, an event expected by the community shortly after the first year of marriage. If a child is not born to a newly married couple, people will call each spouse a "beau-stag" (my spelling), a term of derision which indicates not only sterility but also inability to achieve complete adulthood. In such circumstances, the man will try to have a child by another woman; if he is successful, people will drop the uncomplimentary term. Subsequently, the husband is likely to give part of his earnings to the mother of his child rather than to his wife, undoubtedly causing resentment and therefore producing a situation which may lead to a separation. Since the wife does not have a child that needs support, no economic barriers prevent her from leaving her husband. If after a separation the wife has a child by another man, the community will stop calling her a beau-stag.

On the other hand, a man who fathers a child every year is called a "double-luck," a term of praise. Men believe that siring several children is a sign of their masculinity; in contrast, many women are content to have just one child. Although some women have many children, this is not to be interpreted to mean that fertility per se is an important value; rather it is an indication of the strong desire for frequent sexual intercourse on the part of both men and women. Even though the use of contraceptives is known to most men, they do not use them when having intercourse with their wives. Such knowledge, which is probably learned while on the contract in the United States, is not imparted to women.

During menstruation certain "veins" are believed to be open and to remain partially open for three successive days. Men refer to them as "filthy days" or "run-over days." In contradiction to medical knowledge, it is believed to be easy for a girl to become pregnant during this time because the veins are open. Although because of the "filthiness" men prefer not to have intercourse with a menstruating woman, no belief, such as fear of blood, prevents them from doing so. In fact some women, especially if they are receiving pay from a man, will not tell him they are menstruating. It is not believed necessary that the veins be open in order for a woman to become pregnant. One man told me that a girl could become pregnant before her first menses. This is physiologically possible in a society in which some young girls lead a sexually active life, for a girl might become pregnant on her first ovulation and hence miss her first period.

One man worked out the following system for determining a woman's fertile periods, but I did not discover how closely the elements of this system correspond to beliefs existent in Bahamian society. According to him, the best time to impregnate a woman is the three days just after the five menstrual days. These are followed by three days when she cannot become pregnant, then three days when she can, finally by three days when she cannot, and so on until her next menstrual period. Since the man believes that a child is not born in nine months but in nine moons, he can count nine moons from the three days when he believes his wife conceived in order to calculate when his child will be born. If the child is not born on one of these three days, he will not expect it on the next three days, but on the following three. He claims that the system has proved to be correct for all four of his children. According to his theory, most women menstruate at the beginning of a new moon; thus if the system is correct, most women will become pregnant during the same recurring three-day periods. The man found evidence for the theory in radio broadcasts, for most births are announced during three-days periods, interspersed by three-day periods of relatively few births.

The following positions are used in sexual intercourse. Married couples use positions with the woman lying on her back or with the partners lying on their sides facing each other. When the woman is pregnant, she assumes a stooping position with the man standing behind her. Engaged couples prefer a position in which the girl sits astride the boy because it permits them to part quickly in case of discovery. When a man is having a casual affair he prefers a position that provides maximum enjoyment even though it may be uncomfortable for the woman. Such a position is "The Buck": the woman lies on her back with her legs over the man's shoulders; the man lies on top of her with his arms wrapped around her legs and grasping her shoulders.

A man may have intercourse with his wife up until the night before she delivers because it is believed that the penis helps spread the opening through which the baby's head must come. Of course, the man must be careful at such a time and use a posterior or lateral position. The "come" also helps because it makes for a big, healthy baby. The healthier the husband, the more efficacious the ejaculation is believed to be. It is for this reason that when a large, healthy baby is born people feel sure the father has had frequent intercourse with the mother. Women vary as to whether they want to have sex relations when they are pregnant. When the wife does desire such relations it is believed to be because the fetus wants her to have intercourse. Only in such cases will the baby be big and healthy when it is born.

During pregnancy a woman should be careful of what she does and says so that she will not "mark" her child. If she should look at a picture of a lame or disfigured person, the baby will be born lame or disfigured. If she desires something and then touches part of her body, the baby will be marked with an image in the same place. For example, one woman said she wanted a sapodilla and touched her eye. When her daughter was born there was a brown spot in the white of her eye. Another woman had a feeble-minded daughter because she beat and cursed a "dumb" woman. (For additional examples see Parsons 1918: 144-145.)

There are several indicators which tell a woman whether she is going to have a boy or girl. If there is a blue vein on the mother's abdomen which reaches her navel, the child will be a girl; if the vein goes beyond, it will be a boy. One woman said a black mark on the abdomen was a sign of a boy. The position of the fetus is also believed to forecast the sex of a child. A girl will be on the right side of the mother, a boy on the left. A woman can tell which side the baby is on, because severe pain will prevent her lying on that side. A male fetus will turn over at four months, a female at five months. Several informants said other people felt that a boy gives more pain before birth, but they themselves asserted that it was the "same one pain" as a girl causes.

Some husbands "breed" (have morning sickness) for their wives during their pregnancy. In such cases it is the man who has the nausea and vomiting while his wife remains well. These symptoms go away one or two months before the wife has her baby. The woman then becomes sick shortly before the baby is born, the man remaining well for the period preceding and following the birth. On the other hand, many women are very sick during the time of pregnancy, perhaps because of lack of adequate medical attention. One woman who has had many children said she had a bad headache for eight months before her last child was born, and the morning sickness which has accompanied her last few pregnancies has been more painful than the earlier ones.

Women consider "mishaps" (miscarriages) which occur after the fifth month—the approximate time when the sex of the baby is believed to be recognizable—to be children. Thus when a woman enumerates the number of children she has had who have died, she is apt to include miscarriages. Of course, if she had induced the miscarriage herself she would definitely keep her actions a secret, not only from the census-taker but also from her husband or lover. One way of causing an abortion is to drink a poisonous "bush medicine"; naturally, no woman would tell me how to make such a drug. Moreover, abortion—probably because the fetus is considered a human being—is believed to be murder, a crime so heinous that it results in the loss of one's soul. It would be virtually impossible to ascertain the extent of abortion if it were not for the practice of deathbed confessions as a means of preparing oneself for the afterlife. I was told by several informants that deathbed confessions of abortion frequently occur. In such cases the woman had been impregnated by a man other than her husband. As will be described in the next chapter, some women have lovers when their husbands are away for several months. Abortion is a means of preventing their husbands from learning of the affair and then leaving them.

Delivery. Because they believe that the midwives take better care of them than the nurses, the women of Long Bay Cays prefer to have their babies at home on the island rather than at the hospital in Nassau. One woman prefers to remain on Andros even if it means being separated from her husband. Another informant said she heard of a woman who was left for several days on the delivery table. In another case, she said that a mother and her baby were allowed to fall on the floor.

Female informants said that there was no lessening of pain in childbirth with subsequent deliveries; consequently, a woman does not want any more children after the first. Some women have so much pain that they "lose their senses and try to kill their child." I was told that one woman killed her baby by throwing it down. However, the midwife may even try to sharpen the pain by giving the woman gin or turpentine in order that she will try harder to deliver the baby. A woman usually lies on her back on a bed when giving birth.

Usually no men attend the delivery because "most women do not want men to look upon their naked bodies." One informant was even unwilling to have a doctor in attendance. However, a man may be called if a strong person is needed to hold the woman. For example, one girl was in such pain that she wanted to kill her baby, and it was necessary to call the schoolteacher, a large, powerful man, to restrain her. Another woman who has had seventeen children would always delay delivery until her husband came from the fields so that he could help hold her. Often just the midwife and the woman are in the room, but the woman's mother or another relative may help. Also the midwife may have an assistant who is learning her art.

When the baby is born, the "birth" breaks open. Two women claimed that they could actually hear it tearing. The midwife "catches" the newborn baby in both hands, and takes care of it before the mother. A "meatlike" substance *(vernix caseosa)* is cleaned from the baby's body with soap placed on a soft white cloth and water.

The navel is then dressed. The midwife measures one and one-half joints of the middle finger from the abdomen along the "navel string" (umbilical cord) and ties it as tightly as possible with a waxed flour-sack string before cutting the cord with a pair of scissors. Care must be taken that the cord not be cut too short lest the baby bleed to death. The piece of cord extending beyond the tied string is folded back and twisted; next baby powder is put on the navel, and a large bandage is wrapped around the waist and abdomen. Every morning the navel is redressed by sprinkling it with powder. In about eight days the remainder of the umbilical cord drops off. The bandage should be kept on six to nine months just to make sure no "wind" gets into the navel, since this will cause the baby to cry and the navel to swell. To remove the band early permits wind in the navel and also weakens the back. If the navel should swell, it will remain big and long and people will consider it unsightly. As an extra precaution to prevent swelling, a flattened lead fishing sinker may be placed in the bandage over the top of the navel. A large navel can be caused not only by a careless midwife but also by being "passed by the blood," for large navels are said to run in some families.

After dressing the navel, the midwife sterilizes her fingers by dipping them in rum before continuing her duties. In order to ensure that the baby will talk correctly, she shapes the baby's mouth by pulling its cheeks and "sets up the jawbone" by pushing up on the roof of the mouth. In order not to cut the mouth with a fingernail, the midwife trims her nails very short and as an extra precaution wraps her thumb with cloth. If she should cut the baby with a fingernail, a "pimple" (infection) is apt to form. Following the shaping of the face, the sides, front, and back of the baby's head are pushed together and upward with the hands, to prevent the head from becoming long and, according to local notions, ugly. This measure is also an attempt to close the veins and the fontanelle, for if the veins should remain open, wind might get into them. (I was never told what the wind would do.)

The baby is now put aside while the mother is attended. The latter will try to expel the placenta herself by straining. In order to aid its extrusion a tennis shoe may be rubbed down her back.

One woman, as her first baby was being born, yelled, "Praise God!" Her mother told her not to shout yet, since the "birth" was still inside and must come out or she would die, something which she had not been told before. If the afterbirth does not come out, the midwife puts her hand up inside the womb and tries to remove it. Her hand is wrapped with black cloth, the preferred color because it less readily shows stains. Up to a yard and a half of cloth may be used. After the placenta is expelled, the woman gets out of bed and stands on the floor. The midwife, who is standing in front of her, puts a cloth between her legs and pulls up as tightly as possible, the cloth being kept in position while she lies down on the bed. Another bandage is then wrapped tightly around the waist and fastened with strings or pins.

When a woman is giving birth she is partly covered by her nightgown so that wind does not get into her veins through her vagina. If her nightgown becomes soiled, it is changed. The woman is "put back together" again by pushing the arms and legs up and back. The upper ribs are also pushed, but not the lower waist. Next the woman is rolled over on her abdomen and pressure is applied to her back. Since the veins of the head are believed to be wide open, the scalp is manipulated in the same manner as the baby's head. The midwife blows into one of her hands and slaps it down on the other hand before straightening the woman's toes and fingers. These are pulled until the sockets crack in order to "put back the joints," which are open. The midwife's breath also helps to do this. Next she washes the mother's breasts and lets the child nurse.

The afterbirth is buried in the mother's yard in a deep hole dug by the midwife, with the umbilical cord coiled and laid on top of the sac. A big rock is placed on the hole so that animals cannot dig up the afterbirth. It may also be buried beside a tree, for the tree, like the rock, acts as a marker. Since the spot is not sacred, no one objects if the rock is accidentally removed later.

Consequently, a person may know only that his "navel string" is buried somewhere in his mother's yard. A tree is never planted in the hole, as it is in Jamaica (Beckwith 1929: 56), because of the belief that a tree planted there would not bear fruit. The yard in which a person's navel string is buried is referred to as his "birth place." A person often dreams about his "birth place" because his navel string is buried there. The piece of the umbilical cord that drops off the navel about eight days later is buried in the same place, according to a midwife; one woman did not know what happened to it; another said it could be used to make a bitter tea. The black cloth, which may be used to remove the birth, and the other soiled items are either buried or thrown in the toilet. People were surprised when I asked if any of these items could be used for "obeah" (black magic).

Even though the caul can be used as a medicine or as a means to keep spirits away from the child, the reaction of many people indicated that they had never considered its use for "obeah" as a possibility. If the baby is born with a caul over its face it will be able to see "spirits." (Other people can also see spirits.) The caul is lifted off the face and spread over a hat crown to dry for one day. One midwife said it was put back over the baby's head to dry. The dried caul is put away in a box or jar for the mother to use later if the child is sick or bothered by spirits. It will not rot—in fact, it even remains elastic. A parched and fragmented caul can be used to wash the baby's face, and, like the navel string, it can be made into a bitter tea. A third use is to place it in a little bag which is worn around the child's neck. All three customs can be used both for curing sickness and for preventing the child from being bothered by spirits.

In contrast to many peasant or tribal peoples, Andros Islanders do not attach any particular significance to twins. One woman who has two sets of twins has never heard of any beliefs or customs concerning twins. Elsie C. Parsons (1916: 47) was also unable to record any such beliefs.

In Long Bay Cays the midwife's fee is £2 or £3. It is higher in other places. A woman learns to be a midwife from her mother or by being an assistant to someone who knows the art. There is difficulty, however, in becoming an assistant when one is young; people do not want a girl brought along, for she is more likely than a woman to gossip about what she sees. Usually the assistant is an older woman who has had children.

For the first nine days after the child is born, the midwife comes to the house and bathes the baby with water and alcohol. She shapes the head the way she did when the child was born and stretches the baby daily by holding it up by its legs, by its arms, and by the roof of its mouth. The midwife performs the last operation by inserting her fingers in the child's mouth—they have first been dipped in alcohol—and then suspending the child from outstretched arms. Three days after her delivery, the mother gets up and takes a bath in a tub, goes into the front room for a few moments, and then back into the bedroom for six more days. During this time only close relatives visit the mother and child.

On the ninth day both mother and child come out of the house after having been bathed by the midwife, who is paid on this day. At this time a ceremony called "putting out the baby" is performed, thus introducing the child to the world. The baby is placed on a mat, pad, or cloth which is on the ground. Some woman goes and picks up the baby, and she becomes the godmother. A woman may ask to be the godmother before the baby is born, or someone will be asked by the parents. If no one has been selected beforehand, any woman can go and pick up the baby. The godmother carries the child around while she sings three times, "Thank God, I find one baby." Then she says three times, "Who wants this baby?" The baby is held at arm's length in the direction of the four corners of the earth in this order: east,

65

west, north, and south. The godmother walks around the house holding the baby up, and then goes into the house and gives the baby to its mother. After the ceremony, the father has a party which anyone can attend, with liquor, soft drinks, cookies, and candy provided for the guests.

If a child dies before it is nine days old, it will be buried by the midwife in a little coffin in the graveyard. If the child dies after the ninth day, the burial society the parents belong to provides for the funeral. If the child should become sick when it gets older, it is the "granny's" (midwife's) duty to go and do what she can for the child. In turn, the "granny child" should at times take water, food, groceries, fish, or wood to its granny.

In the "old days" women stayed in the house and avoided hard work for three to six months after the baby was born. They did no cooking or washing, but they might do light chores like sweeping, sewing, and getting out food. But not all women could follow this rule; some had to go out and work in fields in order to earn a livelihood. Today women resume all their duties about one month after delivery. Although the midwife will tell the mother not the have intercourse for three months, the husband will often insist on resuming coitus after two months.

Chapter III

The Mating System

A DOUBLE STANDARD of sexual morality regulates the behavior of men and women. In order to claim adult status a man must have premarital as well as extramarital sex relations, for Andros Islanders believe that the biological nature of the male compels him to have sexual intercourse with as many women as possible. This drive is expected to manifest itself in adolescent males. If a boy does not begin to have coitus by his late teens, people will begin to wonder if he is a "sissy" (homosexual). Most young men, however, live up to community expectations—behavior which is expressed in the saying: "Boys are like dogs." On the other hand, the girl is expected to remain a virgin until the time she has intercourse with her fiancé, and after her marriage to remain faithful to her husband.

Establishing an Extra-residential Union. Whether a man is single or married, he initiates a love affair in the same manner. A dance is considered the best place to find a woman who might be willing to have sexual intercourse. Such women are usually separated or widowed, or have illegitimate children. After talking with the woman for a few minutes, the man may say, "How about a little fun?" Even virgins understand this Bahamian expression. If interested, the woman arranges a meeting place, often her own home. They attempt to conceal the rendezvous from the other dancers in order to protect the woman's reputation. If they are discovered, the blame is invariably placed on the woman, since she has the option to refuse. Rape, seduction with the assistance of alcohol, and love magic are not part of Bahamian culture. The woman, however, does not always take the passive role; she may

67

assume the initiative by having a friend tell the man that she "loves" (desires) him.

A first meeting such as this may develop into an extra-residential union. If the "sweethearts" (lovers) continue to see each other, rights and duties will become established. The man is expected to give presents, usually money, to his "sweetheart," and if a child is born, to help support it. In turn, she must remain faithful to him. If she fails to do this, the community will not condemn him for beating her; her new sweetheart is immune to attack, the blame for unfaithfulness resting entirely on the woman. Extra-residential unions sometimes attain enough stability to persist for years.

Attitude of Wives. If the man is married and his wife learns he has a sweetheart, she may quarrel with him. This will not, however, prevent a husband from having affairs. Since some women realize this, they develop tactics for keeping their husbands faithful. A wife is without legal recourse for terminating her husband's love affairs, for, in contrast with her husband, a wife cannot get a divorce for adultery under Bahamian law. The only grounds available to her are "incestuous adultery," "rape," "sodomy," "bestiality," "adultery coupled with such cruelty" as would allow a "judicial separation," and "adultery coupled with desertion" for two or more years (*The Statute Law*: 617).

The following example illustrates the extent of one woman's attempts to break up her husband's extramarital union, and reveals the stability of both marital and extra-residential unions.

Mrs. Johnson learned of her husband's love affair when she discovered a love letter which had been sent by his sweetheart, a single woman who lived with a younger sister. From that time she tried to keep track of her husband's whereabouts, hoping to catch him with the woman. One night when she learned that he had gone to the woman's house, Mrs. Johnson broke in on the couple and shouted at her husband, "I told you I'd lay hands on you." Mr. Johnson grabbed his wife in order to prevent a fight between the two women, but his sweetheart hit her and ordered her out. Mrs. Johnson broke loose from her husband and struck his paramour yelling, "Don't tell me to go away when you got my man in here!" She chased her husband out of the house, beating and cursing him all the way home. A neighbor tried to intervene but to no avail. Mrs. Johnson attempted to "knock" her husband off the road and into a sink hole filled with water. He retaliated by pushing her into a bush. The next day everyone in the village knew about the fight, to Mrs. Johnson's satisfaction as she wanted to shame her husband. A few days later when she saw her husband's sweetheart going through the village, she went down to the road and cursed her at great length so that all the village could hear. The woman laughed at her. The fight, however, failed to disrupt the love affair. In order to deceive his wife Mr. Johnson now meets his sweetheart in another village. Mrs. Johnson, still suspicious, tries to maintain a constant vigilance over her husband's activities.

Mrs. Johnson will not leave her husband, because she needs his support for herself and her children and also because she loves him. Mr. Johnson knows this and therefore makes no attempt to stop visiting his sweetheart. His wife's belligerent behavior serves only to make him plan his future rendezvous more carefully. His sweetheart wishes to continue the relationship because she is fond of him and needs the small sums of money he gives her. Mrs. Johnson's "rowing" only accomplished the venting of her pent-up hostilities and the disruption of domestic harmony.

Women in similar circumstances who do not quarrel with their husbands rationalize by assuming that it is unreasonable to expect husbands to be faithful, since men are by nature promiscuous. Even the Bible is believed to sanction such behavior, for one often repeated phrase is said to have a Biblical reference: "Man say as many women as he could get he due to have, woman say only one." Also, many wives are fearful that their husbands may desert them if they are openly aggressive. One alternative for the wife is competing with the husband's paramour by making herself more attractive. Another possibility is the use of coercion—refusing to clean and cook until he promises to abandon his sweetheart. However, none of these procedures dissolve extra-residential unions—at most they may serve to delay the husband's immediate return to his sweetheart. Despite all the wife's effort, neither "rowing" nor conciliation prevents the married male from having love affairs.

Attitudes of Husbands. No man will permit his wife to have a sweetheart. If he finds his wife entertaining a man in their home, the husband will assault the lover. However, if the wife is in another man's house, he will retrieve her, but will not attack the other man. The wife, not her lover, is always blamed for the affair; and in both situations the wife will be beaten and deserted by the husband. Therefore wives have sweethearts only when their husbands are away, and, as previously described, many men are away from Long Bay Cays for long periods. If upon his return a man discovers definite evidence of his wife's unfaithfulness, such as pregnancy, he leaves her. When this occurs, as in the follow example, the woman of necessity will continue to have sweethearts.

Mrs. Rolle, who had six children by her husband, became pregnant by another man while her husband was in the United States earning money to improve their home. When he returned and discovered her condition he left Long Bay Cays. Since then she has become the sweetheart of another man (not the father of her seventh child), and has had two children by him. This man helps support her and his two children. His own wife, who has never had a child, fights with him and curses Mrs. Rolle.

A man can demand faithfulness from his wife only if he provides financial support. If the husband fails to send money home during his absence, he has no right to insist on his wife's faithfulness. As has already been pointed out, men give presents, usually money, to their sweethearts. If a husband does not support his wife, she may find it necessary to have a sweetheart in order to get enough money to provide for her children. The following case illustrates what the outcome may be if the husband has not been supporting his wife.

When Mr. Forbes was away from Long Bay Cays for two years, he stopped contributing to his wife's support. In his absence she had a child by another man. When he returned he fought with his wife, but did not leave her. This illegitimate child has remained in their house with her half-brothers and sisters. If Mr. Forbes had been supporting her, he would never have stayed, for the community would have ridiculed him.

SEPARATION

Separation is defined by Bahamians in economic rather than spatial terms. As long as a man continues to support his wife, he is not considered separated from her, although he may stay away from Long Bay Cays for several years. Since most men periodically send money to their wives when they are away, very few persons can be classified as separated. According to the census taken in the four villages, only six men and six women can be thus classified (Table 11). (Since two of the men and three of the women are now involved in consensual unions, Table 12 lists only four men and three women as separated.) Only one man in the census has had a divorce, which he was able to get because his wife admitted her adultery to the court. He later remarried in the United States, but since his wife would not leave, he returned to the Bahamas without her. For this reason he is listed as twice separated. Separations following consensual unions are not included, nor are couples once separated who are now together.

In cases of separation the house is left to the woman, for the people of Long Bay Cays believe that a house is built for the wife

71

TABLE 11

NUMBER OF SEPARATIONS OF MARRIED ADULTS

	Number of Separations			
Age Group	0	1	2	Totals
0-25				
Male	7	0	0	7
Female	9	0	0	9
26-50				
Male	31	1	1	33
Female	38	0	0	38
51-75				
Male	18	4	0	22
Female	21	6	0	27
76-100				
Male	2	0	0	2
Female	2	0	0	2
Totals:				
Male	58	5	1	64
Female	70	6	0	76

TABLE 12

DISTRIBUTION OF POPULATION BY AGE AND CONJUGAL CONDITION

Age Group	Single	Married	Widowed	Consensually Cohabiting	Separated	Totals
0-10						
Male	61	0	0	0	0	61
Female	68	0	0	0	0	68
11-20						
Male	35	0	0	0	0	35
Female	37[a]	3	0	0	0	40

TABLE 12 (continued)
DISTRIBUTION OF POPULATION BY AGE AND CONJUGAL CONDITION

Age Group	Single	Married	Widowed	Consensually Cohabiting	Separated	Totals
21-30						
Male	6	10	0	0	0	16
Female	4[b]	14	0	0	0	18
31-40						
Male	0	9	0	0	1	10
Female	1	10	0	0	0	11
41-50						
Male	0	19	0	0	1	20
Female	0	16	3	2	0	21
51-60						
Male	0	9	1	2	1	13
Female	0	6	4	1	2	13
61-70						
Male	0	2	2	2	1	7
Female	0	1	8	2	0	11
71-80						
Male	0	0	1	1	0	2
Female	0	0	4	0	1	5
81-90						
Male	0	0	1	0	0	1
Female	0	0	1	0	0	1
91-100						
Male	0	0	1	0	0	1
Female	0	0	0	0	0	0
Totals:						
Male	102	49	6	5	4	166[c]
Female	109	50[d]	20	5	3	188[e]

[a] Includes 3 unwed mothers.   [b] Includes 2 unwed mothers.
[c] One male omitted; no data.
[d] One married woman included whose husband is never in Long Bay Cays.
[e] One female omitted; no data.

and the children and so rightfully "belongs" to them. Theoretically the man could get a divorce and retain his house if his wife has committed adultery; but since the conviction that the wife is entitled to the home for the purpose of rearing his children is strong, the husband is unlikely to invoke the law. Furthermore, community sentiment would be arrayed against him, and he would find it unpleasant to remain there.

For three reasons separation is uncommon. (1) Marriage is considered to be permanent and final, separation itself often being looked upon as a temporary arrangement and not as a step toward divorce. A couple separated for several years may resume their marital relationship. (2) Temporary male absenteeism prevents the development of serious marital conflicts. If a "row" does occur, the man can leave for work. When he returns months later, the trouble may have been forgotten. (3) Since extramarital relations are not prohibited to the male, a husband may obtain sexual gratification without the dissolution of the marital bond.

When separations do occur, it is usually for one of three reasons. (1) If a husband is supporting his wife and she has a child by another man or he has proof that she has a sweetheart, he will leave her. (2) If the woman cannot have children for her husband, they may separate at any time. For example, one man has children by several women but none by his wife. Apparently the economic dependence of the husband upon the wife maintains the union; the wife owns part of their home in Long Bay Cays and also half of their house in Nassau. (3) A fight involving a serious economic problem will usually result in separation. The following example describes such a case.

Mr. Strong sent money to his wife for her to buy land on which to build a house. (I was unable to find out why he had married her before building a house.) Her mother contributed some of the money and had the deed put in her name. When Mr. Strong returned from the United States, he built a clapboard house on the land. Later the mother-

74

in-law and his wife drove him off the property. He and his wife have been separated for many years now.

OUTSIDE CHILDREN

The Outside Child. "Outside children" are children of unwed mothers or illegitimate children of married women; the term corresponds to the legal definition of illegitimacy. If, however, the unwed mother marries the putative father of her child, the child is legitimized provided neither of the parents was "married to a third person when the illegitimate person was born" (*The Statute Law:* 1432). Thus the children discussed under "Premarital Pregnancy" in Chapter II are now legitimate although people still refer to them as being outside children. In the population of 356 there are 172 children 15 years old and under; of these children 55 (32 per cent) are illegitimate. (Four of the legitimized children are under 15 years old; they are not included with the 55 illegitimate children.)

There is no prejudice against an illegitimate child. I never heard of a child's being addressed or referred to as a bastard, a term known to nearly all but never used in any situation. Rather, the term used is "outside children" or "jitney." The mother, not her child, is blamed for the transgression. Nevertheless, an outside child is at some disadvantage. He cannot inherit property unless a will is left naming him. But since property is of little value (fields are used without leasing and old houses are nearly worthless), a person of illegitimate birth has little to gain from a will. On the other hand, the child suffers if he has no father to protect him from other children, and one who is living with a grandmother is at a greater disadvantage, since he does not have even his mother's protection. For example, one day on the way home from school, several girls beat up another girl who lives with her grandmother. Finally, a woman who is a distant relative of all these children stopped the fight, threatening to beat them if they did not let the girl alone. She later told me, "Children without parents here have a hard time of it." An outside child is, then, not in a disadvantageous position because he is illegitimate, but because under the social system he has no protector.

The names of children—both legitimate and illegitimate—are recorded and sent to Nassau. The recorder will copy whatever name the mother tells him, although this procedure is not in accordance with the law: "The registrar shall not enter in his register the name of any person as father of such a child [illegitimate] unless at the joint request of the mother and of the person acknowledging himself to be the father" (*The Statute Law:* 1394). The recorder (I did not discuss this with him) may be ignorant of the law, may not wish to contravene folk practice, or may simply be careless. Thus the putative father has no way of knowing if a child has been named after him. However, when the child is christened, the father will learn whether the mother intends the child to bear his surname. Even if the man denies the child, as in the following example, he will not attempt to prevent the child from being named after him.

One young man, who denies being the father of a certain child, did not attend church on the Sunday night the christening was to be held. Although he has had intercourse with the girl, he claims he was away from the island when the child was conceived. (Because of the inaccurate knowledge people possess concerning the length of time from conception to birth, his "proof" that he is not the father is not accepted.) At the christening there was some hesitation when it came time to name the child; finally the great grandmother called out the boy's surname.

However, the name given at the christening may not be the name given to the registrar.

The majority of outside children use their putative father's surname. Of the fifty-five outside children in the census, forty-one are called by their father's name, nine by their mother's name, and

76

five by their mother's husband's name. However, when the child becomes older he will make the decision as to whether he will keep or assume his father's name. (In no case was I told that the child's father was unknown.) This will probably be determined by his feelings toward his father. If the latter has helped contribute to his support, he will most likely retain his name.

The Mothers of the Outside Children. If a woman has an "outside" child, she has difficulty finding a husband because not only is she "second rate" in the sense that she has been another man's sweetheart but also she has a child who must be supported. Even though the child will probably be left in the care of the woman's relatives, a man who marries a woman with an outside child never knows when he may have to support it. Since there is not a shortage of females in Long Bay Cays, such a woman is unlikely ever to marry.

A woman with an outside child has essentially one chance of marriage—with the father of her child. Such marriages frequently happen; one-fourth of the married couples had at least one child prior to marriage. In some cases the birth of the child was probably not preceded by an engagement. Whether or not the woman marries the father of her child depends to a great extent upon the nature of the relationship between them. If the union was the result of a chance meeting at a dance, or if the woman has illegitimate children by other men, or if the father is already married, a marriage is unlikely. However, if the man is single and if the relationship attains such a degree of stability that it can be designated as extra-residential mating, marriage might result.

Whether or not the woman marries, her outside children will probably be reared by her mother or another close female relative: 40 of the 55 illegitimate children (73 per cent) are not living with their mothers. The exact whereabouts of these children will be described in Chapter IV. If the mother stays in Long Bay Cays it is difficult for her to support her children unless she is living with

77

her parents, who help provide for both mother and children. But only five mothers, accounting for seven children, are staying with their parents. The mothers of most of these outside children have gone to work in Nassau in order to help support their children by sending some of their earnings to the relatives who are rearing them. Also, outside children are reared by relatives if the mother enters into a marital or consensual union.

The Outside Child and New Unions. It is unusual for either a man or woman to bring a child of a previous union to a consensual or marital union: only three women and two men have done this. Of the five unions, two are consensual. In two of the households the children see very little of their stepparent. One woman frequently leaves her two children with their grandmother or great-grandmother. One man plans to leave his son with his parents when he and his new wife go to a resort island as seasonal workers. None of the children involved in the five unions is legitimate. There are two other households in which the mother's husband is not the child's father. Each of the two women bore a child while separated from their husbands. After their husbands returned, the children continued to live with their mothers. In the one separation, discussed above, the husband had stopped supporting the wife. In the other, the husband left his wife because she did not become pregnant, but while he was gone she had a child by another man. They are now back together, and she has a one-year-old child by her husband.

Children are not brought to a new union, because of the beliefs about interpersonal relationships that would result from the new household combinations. According to Andros people, fathers are not unkind to stepchildren as stepmothers are. If the husband's children, either legitimate or illegitimate, live with them, the wife will neglect these children, giving preferential treatment to her own children. If the oldest legitimate son of the man remains in the home, the wife is likely to create trouble in

78

order to make him leave. Her reason is simple: she wants her husband to make a will favoring her rather than his son. For these reputed reasons a man will not remarry until his children are grown, or he will send his children to live with his relatives. In either case, he will obtain permission from his grown children before remarrying.

Women, too, seldom bring children to new unions, because they believe that doing this would create a situation which has potential built-in conflict. The woman would probably have children by her new mate, who would prefer these children to the older children by another father. Furthermore, he would not want to support another man's children. Although he would not be unkind to his stepchildren, if a quarrel begins he is likely to start shouting that he has done a great deal for his wife, including the rearing of her children by another man. Obviously, one of the reasons people send their children to be reared by relatives is to avoid possible mistreatment of them.

REMARRIAGE

Most remarried people are now over fifty years old (see Table 13); in fact, many were over fifty when they remarried. A man usually chooses a widow of his own age, rather than a young woman who has never been married. The reason is that a "settled woman" will be a better housekeeper and will be faithful to him. There are no cases of bachelors marrying widows. There are six widowers and twenty widows in the population; two men and three women in consensual unions, who are widowed, are not included in these figures. Only four widowers have remarried —fewer than one-half (four out of ten). Only seven widows have remarried—approximately one-fourth (seven out of twenty-seven).

Six reasons why people are not likely to remarry are these: (1) It is easier to cohabit consensually, a wedding not being required. (2) As mentioned earlier, a man gets permission from his children to remarry, and they may not agree to their father's choice. (3) If a woman remarries, she loses her dower (i.e., her life share of her husband's property). (4) As women get older their mobility increases. Only older women, particularly widows, may visit bars; young women are expected to stay at home. Since many older men and women congregate in bars, companionship is available to both sexes without remarriage. (5) Widows can obtain sexual gratification without remarrying, since the double standard for sexual behavior breaks down when a woman becomes a widow. She can have love affairs and receive financial help for distributing her favors and not be censured by the community. (6) Many women prefer to remain household heads.

TABLE 13

NUMBER OF MARRIAGES OF ADULTS

Age Group	Number of Marriages			Totals
	1	2	3	
0-25				
Male	5	0	0	5
Female	7	0	0	7
26-50				
Male	31	1	0	32
Female	37	0	0	37
51-75				
Male	17	2	1	20
Female	22	6	0	28
76-100				
Male	2	1	0	3
Female	1	1	0	2
Totals:				
Male	55	4	1	60
Female	67	7	0	74

CONSENSUAL COHABITATION

When separation occurs the wife retains control of the house and the husband leaves. If either the man or woman seeks a new partner, the only mating alternatives are extra-residential or consensual unions. As indicated in Table 12, only five couples are cohabiting consensually. The last three reasons why people do not remarry probably also account for the lack of consensual unions. Such unions occur between older people, either widowed or separated, who prefer the companionship of the opposite sex to living alone.

In one consensual union, the woman is a widow, and the man, who recently came from Jamaica, has traveled widely and had a number of wives and mates in the countries in which he has stayed (he is not listed in Tables 12 and 13). In another union both the man and the woman are separated from their former spouses. In a third, the man is a widower and the woman is separated. In all three of these unions, two of them recently formed, the woman owns the house in which she and the man live. The couple who have lived together for a long time have a grandson staying with them and a daughter of the woman. Years ago, before the woman's separation, she had an affair with the man which resulted in the birth of a son—the father of their grandson. Then some years elapsed before they began cohabiting. None of these unions can be converted into marriages, because at least one person in each is separated.

The fourth union, long-established, has resulted in the birth of children. According to the "wife," her "husband" had three "friends" (her term) who preceded her, each of whom died. She helped rear the young children of his third "wife." The present wife and her brother came to Andros from another island while she was still in her twenties. She was probably able to go and live with the man, then perhaps in his late forties, because she had no

81

parents or kinsmen other than her brother in the area who would have tried to prevent the union. Apparently, the brother did not object to it. The woman told me that her "husband" had taken good care of her; he was at this time a community leader and reasonably well-to-do. Since he is now senile, I was unable to learn why he had not married her or his three previous mates. This is the only consensual union in the census which has all the characteristics of a marital union. The fifth consensual union involves an older man and woman, both separated, who stay with his brother when they are living in Long Bay Cays. Since they are gone so much of the time, there is some question as to whether they should have been included in the census.

When a consensual union is formed, the man usually moves in with the woman, as happened in the first three of the five unions discussed above. The third of these is instructive in that both the man and the woman own houses of comparable size and value in the same village, yet the man closed up his house and moved to the woman's. It seems to be improper for a woman to move in with a man unless he marries her. (The atypical nature of the fourth union suggests that it should not be considered a contradiction of this conjecture.) Perhaps conventions about marriage not only require that a house be provided by the man, but also imply that it would be improper to live in a house owned by the man if the couple were not married. If such a principle was operating, this would explain why, in the third union, the man moved in with the woman rather than vice versa (they could not marry, since she is separated).

I conclude this section by describing a consensual union that I recorded during my first stay in Long Bay Cays:

A government employee, a man twenty-eight years old, had a woman living with him who he claimed was his older cousin. She supposedly had a husband living at the northern end of Andros. Although the villagers did not believe him, he told everyone she was his cousin in order to refute their contention that they were cohabiting. Since they were both from other islands, there is no proof of his allegation. Although they seemed to get along well, sometime after I had left Long Bay Cays in September 1959 she went back to her husband. I do not know what circumstances produced the move.

If one assumes that the couple were cohabiting, the question arises: Why did the man not want people to know this? In the first place, since he held a government job he might have wanted to conceal his status from officialdom. Secondly, I was told that he wished to court a girl in another village. By claiming that the woman living with him was a relative, he was establishing himself as a potential suitor. Even though I cannot rule out these two possibilities, I think that he may have made this claim because young men are not supposed to enter into consensual unions, particularly if they have a job which earns an income sufficient for supporting a wife. Although he did not realize it, his denial of deviant behavior actually served to uphold the normative structure of the mating system.

A Two-Choice Mating System

The mating system of the inhabitants of Long Bay Cays is based on two of the three possible choices in mating delineated by M. G. Smith (1962a): marriage and extra-residential unions. Consensual unions, although common in many areas in the Caribbean and the New World, are unimportant; only separated individuals who cannot remarry cohabit consensually. Since a young man and woman are not permitted to enter into a consensual union, the only mating alternatives open to them are marriage and extra-residential unions. Although the community does not sanction the latter type of union for a young couple, such unions do in fact exist. An engaged couple can be said to be mating extra-residentially when a stable sexual union involving separate residences becomes established following the sending of the engagement letter. Even if his fiancée becomes pregnant, rather than cohabiting consensually the man will wait until his house is finished before marrying, although it may mean that their first child is born out of wedlock.

Once married, the husband will have love affairs and may also succeed in establishing an extra-residential union with a single, separated, or widowed woman. His wife, on the other hand, is not permitted to have a sweetheart. If a man learns his wife is having an affair, a separation results. Separated persons, since they are neither divorced nor widowed, may only mate extra-residentially or cohabit consensually. Widowed persons have all three mating choices open to them. However, if a widowed person should wish to mate with a separated person, only two are permissible. Since separated and widowed persons, for reasons described above, usually prefer not to enter a conjugal union, the frequency of remarriages and consensual unions is low. Therefore, the mating system of the inhabitants of Long Bay Cays is virtually based on two rather than three mating choices.

Chapter IV

The Household

HOUSES

HOUSES ARE NEARLY IDENTICAL except for size. They are box-shaped with white limestone walls and shingle roofs, which give them a structure that can well withstand the impact of late summer hurricanes. Porches, usually of wood, extend across the fronts of some houses. Windows, which seldom have glass panes, are often screened to keep out "varmint" (insects); they are always framed by wooden shutters, usually green, which are closed at night.

House Building. The house lot is usually provided by a young man's father from land that he owns in the village. Although the father does not have to contribute financially to the building of his son's house, the community expects him to provide the lot. Sometimes this land is located beside the father's house, but usually it is elsewhere in the village. If the father has no land, some other relative may provide the lot, or if the youth is already courting a girl, her parents may furnish the land.

After the lot has been selected, the first step in building a house is the preparation of the lime for the walls. A lime kiln, approximately two feet in height and eight feet in diameter, is built around a tree stump. Sticks are tied upright to the stump, then bundles of brush are laid on the ground around the stump. Brush is then scattered over the platform built from the bundles, and oölitic limestone rocks broken into pieces smaller than a man's fist are piled evenly on top. When the wind is calm, the top of the stump is ignited with kerosene. The next day the wood has burned away and all that remains is a pile of smoldering limestone, the rocks having become powdered by the heat. After a month or two of weathering, the lime is ready to use.

The next step is to gather the sand and rocks used to construct the walls of the house. Houses are approximately twenty feet square, though they may be larger if the owner can afford the additional expense. After the corners are marked, one-foot-wide trenches are dug down to bedrock from corner to corner, and wooden planks, eight feet long and a foot wide, are laid along both sides of the trenches perpendicular to the ground. These planks are held in place with crosspieces. Mortar is made by mixing water, sand, and lime; recently, some men have started adding commercial cement to their lime-sand mixture. Rocks are placed in the trenches and between the forms, and mortar is poured over them. When the first level of the wall has hardened, the forms are moved up so that a new layer of rocks and mortar can be laid between the planks. Space is left for doors at the front and back of the house, and for two windows in each wall. Walls are approximately eight feet in height.

After the walls are completed, the roof is added. The most common style is a round (hip) roof: the perpendicular distance from the tie beams to the ridgepole is five feet; the ridgepole is four feet long. Variations in roof styles exist: the bell-shaped roof, with no ridgepole, is pointed; the gabled roof, used only by churches and society halls, has a ridgepole running the length of the building. In the past, houses were thatched with palm leaves; however, current homes have shingled roofs, and thatched roofs of old houses are being changed to shingles. After the roof is completed, the flooring, a wooden platform, is put in; the more affluent may prefer a cement floor.

Most houses in Long Bay Cays have rock and mortar walls. Only a few houses have wooden or clapboard walls, and several old houses at The Bluff still have wattle-and-daub walls. Stone houses are preferred, because they can best withstand storms and hurricanes. No one would think of building a wattle-and-daub house today. The 1953 census lists 779 wooden and 857 stone houses for Andros, with most of the wooden houses being at the northern end of the island near the lumber yards. Most houses are square or rectangular, but it is stylish to have an L- or U-shaped house. Porches are also popular; especially desirable are those with four columns or pillars built from cement.

Rooms and Furnishings. Many houses have four rooms: two bedrooms, a living room, and a dining room. Such a house is likely to be occupied by a nuclear family with children. Some houses, however, have three rooms, with only one bedroom. Others have only one or two rooms. Rooms are separated from each other by thin wooden partitions of the same height as the limestone house walls. There is no relationship between size of house and number of rooms, for the partitions can be easily changed to convert a three-room into a four-room house in order to accommodate an increasing family. The 1953 census for Andros lists the total number of rooms as 4,221. This permits computation of the average number of rooms per house as 2.58—a figure one would expect since some houses have only one or two rooms.

The living room is located in a front corner of the house. It contains straight chairs, possibly a rocking chair or an easy chair, perhaps a bench, usually two small tables with kerosene lamps on them, and often a trunk containing household possessions. Sometimes the living room also contains a bed and serves as a sleeping room for the parents, as an alternative to changing the partitions to make four rooms. Curtains hang from wooden rods above the windows. Newspaper pictures of the British royal family and photographs of friends and relatives are either taped or tacked to the green wooden partitions. Framed pictures hang from nails driven into the white limestone walls. If there is a bed in the room it will be covered with a decorative bedspread and serve as a sofa.

The bedrooms are on the side of the house opposite the living room. Each contains a bed, trunks for storing blankets, sheets, and bedspreads, chests of drawers, suitcases, and a nightstand on which rests a white enamel face pan for washing. A large wash tub, used for bathing, may also be found in one of the bedrooms.

The dining room is located at the back of the house closest to the kitchen hut (a separate building). Meals are served on a plain wooden table to the adult males of the household. The only major piece of furniture in the room is the "safe," a cupboard faced with wire screen, in which food is stored safely away from flies. The mother and children spend much of their time during the day in the dining room, the children playing while the mother goes about her household chores.

The Kitchen. The kitchen is usually a dilapidated house about thirty feet behind the main house. It may once have been the home of the owner's parents or grandparents. Typically, the thatched roof is full of holes, the windows are without shutters, and the walls have partly fallen down. Consequently, the kitchen is usually abandoned during a rainstorm. The fire hearth, a stone platform about one foot high, is located in a back corner. Iron rods used to support cooking pots are held in place above the fire by rocks at either end of the hearth. A small fire made from sticks and coconut husks is used for cooking. Various pots, cans, lids, buckets, and strainers are strewn around the kitchen floor. A mill for grinding corn into meal is fastened to the top of a post, which is driven into the center of the floor.

Sleeping Arrangements. The husband and wife sleep in the living room or in the main bedroom. The baby sleeps with its parents until it is old enough to walk, i.e., about nine to twelve months. Then the baby sleeps with the older children. Weaning occurs at this time. The children sleep in the other bed in the house. If there is not room for all, some have to sleep on the floor, rags serving for a mattress. Boys and girls sleep together until about ten years of age, or until the girls begin to develop breasts. The girls then sleep on the floor of the parents' room, or the boys may be shifted to the living room. Some households buy a third bed if it can be afforded.

Some children wet the bed until they are seven or eight years old. When a child wets the bed, all the children remain there until they learn who is responsible. The parents are then told, and the culprit is forced to sleep on the floor.

The wife wears a nightgown, and also panties if children are apt to come into the bedroom. The husband wears undershorts and perhaps a shirt. Girls wear a night dress or slip, and, when older, panties. Boys wear an undershirt and shorts.

Toilet Facilities. Each bedroom contains a "slop tin," a large, white enamel bucket with a lid. The youngest children always use the bucket at night. Children a bit older get a parent to take them outside, but the child is not taken far from the house; he might become injured by walking on broken bottles in the bush. The oldest children may go outside alone, but if it is raining they will use the "slop tin." At night, as during the day, adults go far from the house to defecate; but many women are afraid of spirits of the dead and will not leave the safety of their homes. Since few houses have outdoor toilets or outhouses, the inhabitants evacuate on the beach or in the backyard behind the house. The latter practice is considered preferable, since the wind, which blows from the sea, will not carry back odors. People wipe themselves with newspapers or soft leaves. Feces are buried in the sand on the beach or in holes in the rocky surface of the backyard; slop tins are emptied into these holes during the day. The half-starved dogs which run loose at night perform an important service to the community as scavengers in keeping the beach and yards free from refuse. During the day people go into the bush to defecate, but males urinate beside the houses.

HEADSHIP AND OWNERSHIP

Two basic types of households are characteristic of the domestic system of Long Bay Cays: those containing a cohabiting man and woman and those containing only an adult woman. The former type will be classified as male-headed and the latter type as female-headed. The discussion of these two household types will begin with an analysis of household headship and ownership, and will be followed in the next section by a description of the economic organization of these domestic groups.

Headship. Since men are the only earners of substantial wages in Long Bay Cays, they dominate in domestic affairs. Most men, as pointed out in Chapter I, earn the cash to support their households by going on the contract or by working in Nassau. Thus in households where there is an adult male present, the man controls the economy of the household. Even if the woman owns the house, the man is director of the household. Therefore, if an adult male lives in a household, it is classified as male-headed. If no adult male is present, the household is of course classified as female-headed. Temporary male absenteeism has no influence on the classification of a household; i.e., a household containing a married couple is listed as male-headed even if the husband is a seasonal migratory worker for nine or ten months of the year.

The concept of the developmental cycle of the domestic group (Fortes 1958), though it oversimplifies the presentation of data, is a useful analytic device for understanding the two major phases in the development of the household in Long Bay Cays. In actuality there are several possible cycles with different phases which any Androsian household can go through (Otterbein 1963a). However, since only the differences between male-headed and female-headed households are now under consideration, it is sufficient to use one cycle which shows the transition from male-headed to female-headed households.

Since most houses are built by young men prior to marrying, most households begin their developmental cycle with a male head. The household remains male-headed until the husband dies or, as occasionally happens, leaves his wife. When the man dies, the house is left to his oldest son. Although the Bahamas still follow the law of primogeniture, the wife is entitled to a dower, which means that she is permitted to retain the house as long as she lives. Most widows continue to live in their home even though their children have grown up and moved away. They do not move in with their children or with other relatives even if their own home has fallen into ruin. At any given time there are always several vacant houses in the community. These vacancies result, in part, from families moving to Nassau on a relatively permanent basis. Since most owners believe that a house lasts longer if it is inhabited, they are willing to allow someone else to live in and take care of the house. An older woman who has had to abandon her home is permitted to live in one of these houses rent-free.

Analysis of census data supports the above interpretation. Seventy-two per cent of the households have male heads, most of whom (64 per cent) are under fifty years of age. Of these heads, 80 per cent are married or cohabit consensually (see Table 14). Only 10 per cent of the male heads are single (i.e., unmarried and living alone) or separated; the remaining 10 per cent are widowers. Only 28 per cent of the households have female heads, most of whom (83 per cent) are over fifty. This preponderance of female heads in the older age ranges results from the high propor-

TABLE 14

CONJUGAL CONDITION OF HOUSEHOLD HEADS

| | Per cent | |
Conjugal Condition	Male	Female
Single or separated	10	17
Marital or consensual union	80	4
Widowed	10	79
Totals	100	100

tion (79 per cent) of female heads who are widows. All but one of the widows in the community are household heads; this widow moved in with her daughter and son-in-law. (Widows who are consensually cohabiting are not counted here as widows.) After the deaths of their husbands, 84 per cent (all but three) of the widows remained in their original home. Three of these old women have now had to move into other houses because their own have seriously deteriorated. Only 17 per cent of the female heads are single or separated.

A widow becomes a household head because she wants to remain in charge of her home. She would not want to move in with a son and place herself under her daughter-in-law, nor would a son-in-law want his wife's mother to move in. Thus the practice of retention of household headship by widows appears to be a social adjustment to avoid living with in-laws. In only one household in the census is a mother-in-law living with her son-in-law; in this instance stress has not resulted, because the husband is away working for nine months of the year. Another household contains an old woman who is senile and needs supervision by her granddaughter; here there is no interaction between the widow and her granddaughter's husband.

Ownership. Anthropological investigation of ownership of house lots presented complications. People make title transfers which do not clearly specify boundary lines, which are not properly witnessed, and which they often have no right to make because they do not legally own the land. Because of the informal or non-legal manner in which most land is transmitted, many people do not have clear titles to their house lots. For this reason census reports did not gather sufficient data to indicate whether land had been purchased, inherited, loaned, or received as a gift. Thus the following analysis of house ownership will not consider rights to the land.

Among the household heads investigated, there are eighteen cases of non-ownership. Ten of the male heads do not own their homes. The only three men who rent are two schoolteachers and the telegraph operator. Since these men will not be residing permanently in Long Bay Cays, they have no reason to build houses. Other men, who do not have regular incomes from government salaries, cannot afford to rent. Another schoolteacher lives in his mother's home, which he will inherit when she dies. She now lives in Nassau. Three houses belong to the women in consensual unions. In the remaining three households, the house belongs to the wife.

Eight of the female heads do not own their homes. One woman informally traded houses with a son. Another woman lives in Long Bay Cays only six months out of the year. Although her husband owns the house, he is not considered the head, because he never lives on Andros. Two women live in houses provided by friends; the remaining four live in houses donated by relatives.

Most household heads (Table 15) own their homes (78 per cent); of these the great majority (85 per cent) also built them. A female head who has been left a house by her husband as a dower is considered its owner and is here classified as the builder.

There are two main reasons for these high correlations. First, people seldom sell their homes even when they think they are

TABLE 15

HOME OWNERSHIP OF HOUSEHOLD HEADS

Household Heads	Number of Heads	Per cent Who Own Homes	Per cent of Owners Who Also Built Homes
Male	61	84	84
Female	24	67	87
All heads ..	85	78	85

leaving the island for a long time. Only two household heads have purchased houses. Reasons why people do not sell include these: (1) since people do not have clear titles to their land, an attempt to sell, especially to a non-relative, might end in a legal quandary, with a number of people making claims to the land; (2) a person who leaves Andros to work in Nassau or the United States may want to return; not selling his house assures him of a place to return to; (3) it is strongly felt that the home really belongs to the wife and children. Even in cases of separation the house is left to the wife. When a man builds a house, he intends to leave it to his offspring. The prevalence of this intention is not refuted by the fact that only six houses were occupied by the adult children and grandchildren of deceased householders. In the second place, a man wants the satisfaction of having built his own home, even though, as pointed out earlier, his family and relatives may have assisted him and even have done part of the construction. Rather than buy a house, or take over an old one and repair it, even if it is his father's, a man prefers to build a new house. If a man has inherited a house, the wooden parts—shutters, doors, partitions, and floor—are likely to be removed and used in the new building.

In summary, the characteristics of male-headed and female-headed households can be easily delineated if a typical household is described in terms of its developmental cycle. A household comes into existence when a couple marries. The young man builds his own home at this time, instead of moving in with anyone or waiting until he can inherit his father's. The lack of available houses prevents him from buying one. The money he has saved while working away from Long Bay Cays allows him to realize his desire to own his own home. Consequently, most male heads not only own their homes but also have built them. During the early phase of the life cycle of the domestic group, the household is male-headed. When the husband dies the wifes continues to live in the house. Since the husband's death usually precedes the wife's (there are six widowers and twenty widows in the census), the household is likely to be female-headed during the latter phase of its cycle. After a few years the house may be in such poor condition that the widow will have to move into an empty dwelling belonging to friends or relatives.

Economic Features of the Household Group

If households are to exist as viable economic units, they must provide each member with subsistence. In order for a household to meet such a requirement, certain economic adjustments which are deviations from the ideal patterns are necessary in the division of labor. After analyzing task participation by age and sex, I shall describe the daily routine and typical meals consumed by a family. The section concludes with a computation of grocery expenditures for both male- and female-headed households.

Division of Labor. A husband is expected to support his wife and children. He does so by growing crops, scale-fishing, crawfishing, working as a carpenter or mason, and helping to build roads. The wife is expected to take care of the house and the children, to do the laundry, to cook meals whenever her husband wants to eat, and to help in the fields when she can. She is also expected to earn a little money by catching land crabs, plaiting (weaving palm strips for baskets), and helping in the shop if she and her husband have one; but during the childbearing period she should stay in the house and busy herself with domestic tasks. The children are assigned a minimal number of chores: weeding, fishing from shore (about the only thing they are willing to do), getting wood and water, running errands, and taking care of younger children.

In actual practice such patterns are not strictly followed. Table 16 lists the tasks performed by the residents of Long Bay Cays and indicates who—by age and sex—participates in each. The jobs men perform when they are working away from Andros are not

TABLE 16

Tasks	Adults		Adolescents		Children	
	Male	Female	Male	Female	Male	Female
Head schoolteacher	*	–	–	–	–	–
Assistant schoolteacher	*	*	*	*	–	–
Nurse	*	*	–	–	–	–
Midwife	–	*	–	–	–	–
Shopkeeper	*	*	–	–	–	–
Bartender	*	*	–	–	–	–
Carpenter	*	–	–	–	–	–
Mason	*	–	–	–	–	–
Preacher	*	–	–	–	–	–
Constable-postmaster	*	–	–	–	–	–
Deputy constable	*	–	–	–	–	–
Telegraph operator	*	–	–	–	–	–
Sea captain	*	–	–	–	–	–
House building	*	*	*	–	–	–
Road building	*	*	–	–	–	–
Shipbuilding	*	–	–	–	–	–
Sponge fishing	*	*	–	–	–	–
Crawfishing	*	–	–	–	–	–
Fishing from vessel	*	–	–	–	–	–
Fishing from dingy	*	(*)	*	–	–	–
Fishing from shore	(*)	*	*	(*)	*	(*)
Catching land crabs	(*)	*	*	*	*	*
Cutting bush on farm land	*	*	–	(*)	–	–
Heaping and burning bush	*	*	–	–	–	–
Planting crops	*	*	–	–	–	–
Weeding and gathering crops	*	*	–	*	*	*
Gathering firewood for home	(*)	*	(*)	*	*	*
Building fire at home	(*)	*	(*)	*	(*)	(*)
Cooking and tending fire	(*)	*	(*)	*	–	–
Washing dishes	(*)	*	(*)	*	(*)	*

TABLE 16 (continued)

Tasks	Adults		Adolescents		Children	
	Male	Female	Male	Female	Male	Female
Carrying water	*	*	*	*	*	*
Laundry and ironing	(*)	*	(*)	*	–	–
Scrubbing floors	(*)	*	(*)	*	–	–
Gathering palm tops	(*)	*	(*)	*	(*)	*
Plaiting	(*)	*	(*)	*	–	*
Butchering	*	–	–	–	–	–
Taking care of small children	*	*	*	*	–	–
Climbing coconut trees	–	–	*	(*)	*	(*)
Tending pigs, chickens, and goats	*	*	*	*	*	*

*=Frequently.　(*)=Occasionally.　–=Seldom.

included. Although most occupations are male-dominated, a woman may be a nurse, a midwife, or an assistant schoolteacher; she may preach but she will not be considered a preacher by profession. She may also help take care of a shop or bar. Women take an active part in construction work by carrying bags of sand and rocks on their heads. The reason adolescents participate little in construction work is that jobs are scarce and are allotted by the project supervisor to the adults of the community. Although fishing is primarily a male task, no taboos or sanctions prevent a woman from participating, nor would doing so be considered unladylike. In the old days a few women were sponge cutters. Farming is performed by both men and women. Since many of the men are away the greater part of the year, providing subsistence falls heavily upon the woman. Domestic chores lie in the woman's domain. The wife is helped greatly by teen-age daughters. The husband may also perform any of these tasks; moreover, some men have reputations for being good housekeepers. Most men do not like to cook; some teen-age boys say cooking is for girls. However, domestic chores are not regarded as unmanly.

97

For economic reasons men and women often perform many of the same tasks. In her husband's absence, the wife must take care of the fields. If the wife is away, is ill, or is having a baby, the husband will take over the household chores. In contrast to many societies, there are no sanctions which enforce a division of labor that permits men to perform only certain tasks and limits women to others. That is, in a normative sense, any one of the tasks on the list may be performed by anyone physically able to do so. The importance to the social system of such a "flexible" division of labor is that a household containing only one adult, male or female, can operate as an independent unit. In a society with a division of labor by sex in which tasks are not interchangeable, female-headed households resulting from the absence of adult males would be an impossibility. The "flexible" division of labor consequently plays an important part in the continuance of female-headed households.

Daily Routine. If the husband is going to the fields, he gets up before sunrise in order to do his work during the coolest part of the day. The wife prepares breakfast upon arising, unless there is a daughter in her late teens who rises before either parent and begins the meal. Breakfast is eaten sometime between 6:00 and 8:00 A.M. It consists of boiled fish, fish soup, eggs, souse (made from the head and insides of a pig), grits, bread, tea, coffee, or some other hot drink. Left-overs from the night before may be finished. Hot cereal is not commonly eaten. After breakfast children leave for school, which starts at 9:00 A.M. The wife does laundry and other household chores during the morning.

When the husband returns from the fields at noon, he may eat a light lunch or snack consisting of left-overs from breakfast, boiled crabs, cassava, yams, potatoes, or fruit. Dinner, the major meal of the day, is eaten when the children return from school after 3:00 P.M. The meal consists of "peas and rice" (the Bahamian national dish), potatoes, yams, casava, or grits. The meat or "relish" is either fried fish, pork, canned meat (probably corned beef), fried chicken (a great delicacy in the Bahamas), boiled crab (often cooked with rice), conch, or minced crab. About the only way to prepare meat is to "smother" it with tomato paste and onions while it is cooking in the frying pan. In fact, food is not believed to be properly cooked until it is "smothered." After dinner the wife cleans up, the children go to play, and the husband goes to talk with his friends, who usually congregate at the bars.

Some time after sunset the family will have supper or "tea." This usually consists of left-overs from dinner, coffee or tea, bread, johnny-cake, or sweet-potato bread. Fruits are not eaten along with meals, but during the day as snacks.

This description of meals makes it clear that there is little variation in the foods consumed or in the manner of their preparation. Culinary experimentation or novelty is unthought of.

Household Expenditures. The minimum cost of the groceries —the largest expenditure of any household—needed to prepare meals for a man, woman, and three children will show why a man must periodically leave Long Bay Cays to work as a wage laborer. The amount of money needed by a female-headed household will also be computed; even though the requirements are minimal for a woman living alone, she must still receive funds from several sources in order to keep the household functioning.

The minimum expenditure for groceries by a couple with three small children for one month is about $15.00 (see Table 17). The man who provided this list said it was representative of other households of the same size. The figure given is minimal; it does not include the amount spent for fresh pork (3*s.* per pound), corned beef (4*s.* per can), fish, fruit, tobacco, soft drinks, or liquor. The amount spent on these less necessary items varies from family to family. The average household (4.2 persons per house) spends from $20.00 to $25.00 a month on food. Chapter I has already described how the lack of jobs in Long Bay Cays and the need for cash to buy groceries and other necessities has produced temporary male absenteeism. A man who periodically leaves the area to work for wages can earn enough to contribute $25.00 or more a month to his family; thus a male-headed household can manage financially, provided the husband occasionally leaves Long Bay Cays.

While the husband is away, if he fails to send money or groceries to his wife, she may have to take a sweetheart in order to help support the household. The financial need of a deserted woman produces a situation which can lead to the establishment of an extra-residential union, for married men sometimes mate with separated women.

As was pointed out in the last section, widows prefer to remain in their own homes rather than move in with kin. They are able to manage financially because of the government old-age pension of £2 a month provided to people over sixty-five years old. One-half of the female household heads are over sixty-five, two-thirds

TABLE 17

Cost of Basic Groceries for One Month
for a Couple with Three Children

Item	Cost per Unit	Rate of Consumption	Cost in Dollars for One Month
Flour	100 lb. bag, £2 6s.	1 bag in 3 months	$2.15
Rice	100 lb. bag, £3 10s.	1 bag in 6 months	1.65
Grits	100 lb. bag, £2 6s.	1 bag in 6 months	1.10
Lard	½ box (28 lbs.), £2	½ box in 3 months	1.80
Tomato paste	1 can, 1s. 9d.	2 cans per week	2.00
Sugar	1 lb., 1s.	5 lbs. per month	.70
Milk	1 can, 9d.	8 cans per week	3.40
Baking powder	1 can, 2s.	1 can per month	.30
Coffee	1 lb., 6s.	3 lbs. per month	2.50
Total Expenditures for One Month			$15.60

of them living alone. If we estimate that an old woman needs $8 a month to live on—perhaps not even this much—evidently the £2 ($5.60) contributed by the government will provide most of her support. If there are grandchildren living with the widow, additional help will be needed. If the parents of these children make a contribution to the running of the house, these female-headed households can survive.

The twelve female heads under the age of sixty-five have difficulty in supporting a household because they do not receive an old-age pension. Nine of them have increased difficulties because they have children staying with them. Therefore they must find means of support if their households are to continue functioning. Four sources of income are open to them. They can sell crops, plaited articles, and land crabs which they have caught. They can take in grandchildren or children of other kin, and use the parents' contributions to support the household. A third possible source of income is gifts, usually money, from lovers who periodically pay them visits. Finally, some children help support their aging mothers. These institutionalized features of the social structure permit the persistence of female-headed households as viable economic units.

HOUSEHOLD COMPOSITION

The mating system of the inhabitants of Long Bay Cays is the most important influence on the household composition of the eighty-five households in the census. The following generalizations show the manner in which certain features of this system produce household types, and their frequencies.

1. Since young men establish their own households upon marriage, there are no extended-family households.

2. Since a household is established when a young couple marries and since most women have several children during their

lifetime, a high percentage of the households consist of nuclear families.

3. Since a person does not usually bring a child of a previous union—usually an outside child—to a marital or consensual union, very few illegitimate children are found in nuclear-family households.

4. Since widowed and separated persons seldom remarry or enter consensual unions, a large number of households contain one adult male or female rather than both.

5. Since one-third of the children are illegitimate and since nearly three-fourths of these children are not living with their parents, many households contain illegitimate children who are not offspring of the household head.

6. Since the mothers or other female relatives of the unwed girls usually rear these children, many households span three generations.

The following analysis of the household composition of the eighty-five households demonstrates that these statements are correct. Particular attention will be devoted to studying the distribution and placement of outside children in the domestic system.

Household Types. In order to analyze household composition one may group the eighty-five households into a limited number of types—types which permit the investigator to study the combinations of members which are meaningful in terms of the social structure. Genealogies of each household were sorted for four major categories: (1) single-person households, which subdivide into those with a male head and those with a female head; (2) childless couples and couples with children fifteen years old and under; (3) households consisting of one parent with children, which separate into those with a mother and those with a father; (4) households with three or four generations subdivided into households with both grandparents, those with only the grandmother, and those with only a grandfather. The procedure gave four basic types and nine subtypes of households which correspond closely to the division made by many Caribbeanists. The subtypes, however, can be regrouped. They can, for instance, be grouped according to the two basic types of households which have been used to analyze the mating system of Long Bay Cays—male-headed (types A1, A2, B1, B3, C2, and D2) and female-headed (types B2, C1, and D1). Subtypes can also be grouped to show the households containing a cohabiting man and woman (types A1, A2, and B1).

Table 18 shows the distribution of households by type. Nuclear-family households contain a couple joined by a conjugal bond, either marital or consensual. Children may (type A1) or may not (type A2) be present. Grandparent households span three generations; the second generation may or may not be present. That is, all three subtypes of type B contain at least a first or grandparent generation and a third generation, usually the grandchildren of the first generation. If there are both an adult male and female in the first generation who are joined by a conjugal union the household is classified as containing both grandparents (type B1). If only a female is present, the domestic unit is listed as a grandmother household (type B2); if only a male, the unit is classified as a grandfather household (type B3). Denuded nuclear families (types C1 and C2) consist of only one parent and a child. They are referred to as denuded because they result from the death or desertion of one of the parents in a nuclear family. This term was first used by Edith Clarke (1957; also Solien 1960). Single-person households (types D1 and D2) contain a man or woman who lives alone. The typology does not include a category for sibling households, since none are found in the census.

The use of the term three-generation or grandparent household rather than extended family is deliberate. In the usual sense an extended family is one in which the eldest son (or possibly the youngest) takes over upon the death of the father. Since sons

103

TABLE 18

Distribution of Population by Household Type

Household Types	No. of Households	Per cent	Adults Male	Adults Female	Children Male	Children Female	Total Members	Per cent	Average No. of Members per Household
A. Nuclear family									
1. With children	25	29	35	28	34	51	148	41	5.9
2. Childless	8	9	8	8	0	0	16	5	2.0
	33	38	43	36	34	51	164	46	5.0
B. Grandparent									
1. Both grandparents	15	18	26	29	31	28	114	32	7.6
2. Grandmother	9	11	6	13	9	12	40	11	4.4
3. Grandfather	2	2	2	0	2	0	4	1	2.0
	26	31	34	42	42	40	158	44	6.1
C. Denuded nuclear family									
1. Mother-child	4	5	0	7	2	2	11	3	2.8
2. Father-child	1	1	1	0	1	0	2	1	2.0
	5	6	1	7	3	2	13	4	2.6
D. Single person									
1. Female	11	13	0	11	0	0	11	3	1.0
2. Male	10	12	10	0	0	0	10	3	1.0
	21	25	10	11	0	0	21	6	
Totals	85	100	88	96	79	93	356	100	4.0

bring their wives to live in the household, such a family has continuity through generations. However, the grandparent household of the Andros Islanders is not of this type. Sons and daughters leave upon marriage. Sons build their own homes, for even if they inherit their father's house, they do not move into it or repair it. The grandchildren in the household are likely to be daughters' children rather than sons' children. They are considered temporary residents: either their mother may take them away at any time, or they leave when they are able to care for themselves. Since it is unlikely that they will inherit anything, houses and land being of little value, they have no reason for remaining beyond the period of their childhood. Therefore a household has continuity for only the life span of the senior generation. For these reasons the grandparent household of the Andros Islanders bears little resemblance to the extended families found in many areas in the world.

Examination of Table 18 shows that 38 per cent of the households are nuclear families, 31 per cent grandparent households, 25 per cent single-person households, and 6 per cent denuded nuclear families. If the subtypes are regrouped by sex of household head, 72 per cent are male-headed and 28 per cent are female-headed. Regrouped in a different way, 57 per cent of the households contain a cohabiting man and woman. Only 11 per cent are headed by a grandmother (type B2); only 5 per cent, by a mother.

Forty-six per cent of the population belongs to nuclear-family households. The remainder is distributed as follows: 44 per cent in grandparent households, 4 per cent in denuded nuclear families, and 6 per cent in single-person households. Male-headed households contain 83 per cent of the population, female-headed households only 17 per cent. Households including a cohabiting man and woman comprise 78 per cent of the population, grandmother households 11 per cent, and mother-child households 3 per cent. Grandparent households are the largest in size, averaging over six members per house. Nuclear families average nearly five members. Denuded families average over two and a half members.

Table 19 shows the composition of households. Only two married children and two daughters-in-law live in male-headed house-

TABLE 19

RELATIONSHIP OF MEMBERS TO HEADS OF HOUSEHOLDS

Categories of Relationship	Number in Household	
	With Male Head	With Female Head
Male Kin:		
Head	61	..
Married son	1	0
Unmarried son	58	4
Son-in-law	0	0
Son's son	5	3
Daughter's son	16	5
Consanguineal kin	1	3
Affinal kin	8	2
Totals	150	17
Female Kin:		
Spouse	48	..
Head	..	24
Married daughter	1	0
Unmarried daughter	67	9
Daughter-in-law	2	0
Son's daughter	3	0
Daughter's daughter	9	5
Consanguineal kin	2	6
Affinal kin	12	1
Totals	144	45

holds. This is definite evidence that children upon marriage set up their own household. Unmarried children number 125; grandchildren, 33. There are only three consanguineal kin of the head other than direct descendants. Affinal relatives (i.e., consanguineal kin of the spouse) total twenty. Thus the vast majority (92 per cent) of the members of male-headed households are the husband and wife, their children, and grandchildren.

In female-headed households, there are no married children, sons-in-law, or daughters-in-law. Again we observe the pattern of children setting up their own households upon marriage. There are thirteen unmarried children and also thirteen grandchildren. Consanguineal kin of the head total nine, affinal kin only three.

The number of grandchildren totals forty-six, of whom thirty-five are daughters' children and eleven are sons' children. Thus there are three times as many daughters' children as sons' children living with their grandparents. This is a definite indication that daughters, whether they live at home or not, involve their mothers in the care of their children. If the number of relatives of the spouse (the twenty affinal kin under male heads), plus the number of relatives of female heads (the nine consanguineal kin under female heads), is compared with the number of relatives of the head (the three consanguineal kin under male heads), plus the number of relatives of the deceased husband (the three affinal kin under female heads), it is apparent that nearly five times (29 to 6) as many maternal relatives as paternal relatives live in the households. Thus other than the heads and their nuclear families who reside in the households, it is the children of daughters and relatives of the wife who constitute the larger proportion of the non-nuclear-family members of households.

Table 20 makes this point even clearer. Over four times as many children (36 to 8) who are not living with either of their parents are living with mother's kin rather than father's kin. The mother's kin includes the mother's mother in three-fourths of the cases (27 out of 36). The table also provides evidence that when the child is living with only one parent, this is almost invariably the mother (21 out of 24).

Distribution of Outside Children. Table 21 shows the distribution of illegitimate children fifteen years old and under by

TABLE 20

RESIDENCE OF CHILDREN NOT LIVING WITH BOTH PARENTS*

Residence	Number of Children	
Parent		
Mother	21	
Father	3	
		24
Mother's kin		
Mother's parents	18	
Mother's father	1	
Mother's mother	9	
Mother's mother's sister	1	
Mother's father's sister	2	
Mother's sister	4	
Mother's brother	1	
		36
Father's kin		
Father's parents	3	
Father's father	2	
Father's mother	1	
Father's father's mother	1	
Father's father's wife	1	
		8
Brother	1	
Total		69

* Data do not include children of men if the child is not living in the four villages; data do include children who are living elsewhere but whose mothers live in the four villages.

household type. Four children who were legitimized after the marriage of their parents are not included. There are five outside children (9 per cent) in nuclear-family households. Forty-nine of the children (89 per cent) are in grandparent households. Only one (2 per cent) lives in a mother-child household. This table indicates that illegitimate children are usually raised in grandparent households, rather than in nuclear- or denuded nuclear-family households.

Only 27 per cent (15 out of 55) of the outside children are living with their mothers. Of these fifteen illegitimate children, nine are living with their mothers in grandparent households (types B1 and B2). (One woman has three children.) Two of these children live with mothers who are cohabiting consensually with the

TABLE 21

DISTRIBUTION OF ILLEGITIMATE CHILDREN BY HOUSEHOLD TYPE

Household Type	Number	Per cent	Number Living with Mothers	Number of Mother-Child Units
A. Nuclear family				
1. With children	5	9	5	3
2. Childless	0	0	0	0
	5	9	5	3
B. Grandparent				
1. Both grandparents	31	56	8	6
2. Grandmother	16	29	1	1
3. Grandfather	2	4	0	0
	49	89	9	7
C. Denuded nuclear family				
1. Mother-child	1	2	1	0
2. Father-child	0	0	0	0
	1	2	1	0
Totals	55	100	15	10

male head of the household. One of the children is in a denuded nuclear family, and the remaining five are in three nuclear families. Thus in contrast to the practice in many areas in the Caribbean, a mother living alone with her outside children is a rarity. There are no households consisting of a mother, her illegitimate daughters, and their illegitimate children as have been reported for some other areas.

Mother-child units are not usually found occupying the second and third generations of grandparent households. Only four daughters and their outside children are living in such households (type B1). The two additional mother-child units shown in Table 21 occupy the first generation. Only one grandmother household (type B2) contains a mother and her son. The fact that most outside children are living in grandparent households without their mothers provides rather conclusive proof that daughters send or leave their illegitimate offspring to be reared by their grandparents or other kinfolk.

Examination of the household composition of grandparent households, from the point of view of the presence of illegitimate children, clearly establishes the fact that one service performed by grandparent households is the rearing of outside children. Of all the children aged fifteen and under living in grandparent households, 61 per cent are illegitimate (49 out of 82). If only non-nuclear-family kin are considered (children of the household head being omitted), the results are even more conclusive (Table 22). Non-nuclear-family kin can be classified according to genealogical connection with the household head: grandchildren, consanguineal kin, and affinal kin. Included in Table 22 are household members older than fifteen, but at least one generation below the household head. Seventy-six per cent of the grandchildren (37 out of 49) are illegitimate; 33 per cent (3 out of 9) of the consanguineal kin are illegitimate; 83 per cent (5 out of 6) of the affinal kin are illegitimate. Thus 70 per cent (45 out of 64) of all non-nuclear-family kin in grandparent households are illegitimate.

Relationship of Household Types to Economic Features. The analysis of the economic features of male-headed and female-headed households indicated that female heads, in contrast to male heads, owned houses which were in poor condition, possessed no property which could bring a financial return, and did not have gainful occupations. Although it would have been possible to verify this contention at that point, the proof has been delayed until now in order that the nine household types could be utilized in the analysis. The procedure followed in demonstrating economic differences between household types consists of constructing an economic index that will permit the ranking of individual households and household types. The method used is derived from the technique developed by W. Lloyd Warner, Marchia Meeker, and Kenneth Eells (1960) for constructing an index (known as the Index of Status Characteristics) to measure an individual's social class. For Long Bay Cays, house type, property, and occupation were found to be suitable indicators for distinguishing economic differences between household types.

The first section of this chapter described the desirability of houses according to certain characteristics of construction. Therefore, census reports included information on these three house

TABLE 22

DISTRIBUTION OF ILLEGITIMATE CHILDREN IN GRANDPARENT HOUSEHOLDS

| Birth Status | Non-Nuclear Family Kin | | | | | | Total | |
| | Grand-children | | Consanguineal Kin | | Affinal Kin | | | |
	No.	Percent	No.	Percent	No.	Percent	No.	Percent
Illegitimate	37	76	3	33	5	83	45	70
Legitimate	12	24	6	67	1	17	19	30
Totals	49	100	9	100	6	100	64	100

features: kind of roof (the term "shingles" here includes tar paper, asbestos, and metal roofing, all of which are better than "thatch"); presence of a porch (of either wood or cement); and construction material (limestone or wood). Another reason for choosing these features was the ease with which they could be observed and recorded. Other characteristics, such as size and condition, are important; however, by using only three attributes or variables, one can limit the number of basic house types to four. The houses listed in Table 23 can be regrouped into the following house types: (I) limestone houses with a porch and shingle roof; (II) limestone houses without a porch and with a shingle roof; (III) limestone houses without a porch and with a thatch roof; (IV) houses constructed of wood. These house types are listed in

TABLE 23

CLASSIFICATION OF HOUSES BY BUILDING MATERIALS

Building Materials	Number of Occupied Houses
I. Limestone	
A. No porch	
1. Thatch	10
2. Shingles	51
B. Porch	
1. Thatch	0
2. Shingles	20
II. Wooden	
A. No porch	
1. Thatch	1
2. Shingles	2
B. Porch	
1. Thatch	0
2. Shingles	1
Total	85

decreasing order of their monetary value. In order to use house type as an indicator in the construction of an index of socio-economic class, three points were assigned to a Type I house, two points to a Type II house, one point to a Type III house, and no points to a Type IV house. In other words, each household was assigned from zero to three points depending upon the type of house it occupied.

The ownership of property provides a scale for measuring observable wealth. Since land, other than building lots or coconut groves, is of little value, no points were assigned for land ownership. One point was assigned for the ownership of each extra house. Possession of a dingy was also given one point. Ownership of a bar, a shop, a society hall, or a sloop conferred two points each. The owner of a club (a bar with a dance hall) or a "smock-boat" (a fishing vessel with a well for keeping fish alive) was assigned three points.

Occupations were grouped into two types: government jobs and trades. Points were assigned in terms of the amount of income derived from the occupation. Those not earning a regular and substantial income were omitted. Government jobs—constable-postmaster, telegraph operator, and assistant schoolteacher —were assigned two points, except for the head-teacher position, which was assigned three points. Trades—mason, carpenter, and sea captain—were assigned one point. If a man was both a mason and a carpenter, he received two points. None of the women in the villages had occupations that entitled them to a ranking on this indicator.

The index used for ranking households was arrived at by combining the three indicators by the addition of points. Since none of the scales was deemed more important than any of the others in the prediction of economic position, they were not weighted. It should be pointed out that it is not individual wealth but that of households which is being measured; the scores of

113

husband and wife, therefore, are computed together. In some cases the wife owns property apart from the husband. For example, one of the households was scored as follows:

Grandparent Household (Type B1)

House type: I	3
Property: shop, dingy, sloop	5
Occupation: mason and carpenter	2
Rank	10

The index was computed for each household; scores ranged from zero to ten. Table 24 shows the average index for each household type.

All the male-headed household types, except for one case of C2, rank higher than any of the female-headed types. The data thus demonstrate that female-headed households hold an inferior economic position within the domestic system.

In the male-headed households, the differences between grandfather (B3) and grandparent (B1) households is of no significance. Both the grandfather households were grandparent house-

TABLE 24

AVERAGE INDEX OF ECONOMIC RANK FOR EACH HOUSEHOLD TYPE

Household Type	Average Index	Total Cases
Grandfather (B3)	6.5	2
Grandparent (B1)	4.5	15
Single male (D2)	4.3	10
Nuclear family, childless (A2)	3.9	8
Nuclear family, with children (A1)	3.7	25
Mother-Child (C1)	2.3	4
Father-child (C2)	2.0	1
Grandmother (B2)	2.0	9
Single female (D1)	1.0	11
Total		85

holds until about two years before the census was taken. When the men's wives died the households became converted into type B3. Since this might have happened in any of the grandparent households, it is purely chance that the difference is as much as 2.0. The combined index for the two types is 4.8. The heads of these households are the leaders and the wealthiest men in the community. Single male households (D2) rank higher than nuclear families because four of the men have government jobs (three schoolteachers and the telegraph operator), and two are widowers who own bars and other property. Single male households are actually of two types: young men yet to marry and older men who are widowers. The former group have an index of 6.0, and the latter an index of 3.2. The difference between nuclear families with and without children is only 0.2, a figure too small to be of any significance.

Of the female-headed households, mother-child households (C1) rank the highest. This is related to the fact that these domestic units occupy better houses than grandmother or single female units. Households of type C1 have an average house type index of 2.0, types B2 have an index of 1.6, and types D1 have an index of 1.5.

If the household types are linked together into a developmental cycle, the index can be used to show the levels of economic well-being of an average household during the phases of its cycle. The typical household begins as a nuclear family without children (index 3.9), shortly becomes a nuclear family with children (index 3.7), and with the addition of grandchildren, who are usually illegitimate, becomes a grandparent household (index 4.8). If the wife dies first the children will probably go to live elsewhere, leaving the man alone in the house (the index for widower households of type D2 is 3.2.). If the husband dies first, which is usually the case, the domestic unit becomes a grandmother household (index 2.0.). When the widow is no longer able to care for outside children she will live alone (index 1.8). Thus a household, while it is male-headed, slowly increases in economic well-being for approximately the first thirty or forty years of its developmental cycle; with the death of a spouse the level rapidly falls, because the old man or woman can no longer repair the house or invest in further property. If the surviving spouse is a widow, the drop is even more rapid. She often keeps the household functioning by rearing the outside children of daughters or female relatives, who usually contribute to the support of the household.

This section has described nine household types. One reason for delineating the types in this manner was in order to understand where children were being reared. In general, legitimate children live with their parents in nuclear family and grandparent households. Illegitimate children live apart from their mothers in grandparent and grandmother households. This distribution of children throughout the domestic system establishes the fact that one of the important services provided by grandparent households is the rearing of outside children.

Chapter V

Interpersonal Relationships

THE SYSTEM OF INTERPERSONAL RELATIONS of the Andros Islanders is based upon relationships of five different types: (1) relationships within the nuclear family household; (2) relationships within the grandparent household; (3) consanguineal relationships outside the household; (4) affinal relationships; and (5) fictive kin relationships. The procedure followed in analyzing these relations consists in describing both the ideal and the actual behavior between kinsmen and the terminology which accompanies the relationships.

RELATIONSHIPS WITHIN THE NUCLEAR-FAMILY HOUSEHOLD

Husband—Wife. The relations between husband and wife have already been described in some detail. In general the relationship is based upon cooperation and affection. In contrast to the practice in some Caribbean islands, particularly those with a Spanish cultural tradition such as Puerto Rico (Landy 1959: 79), the husband helps the wife with domestic chores wherever possible; she in turn does as much hard work as she is able. Such cooperative behavior seems to produce in most families strong affective ties between husband and wife.

Before discussing terms used by husband and wife in addressing each other, I shall describe the use of names. Bahamians refer to the parts of a person's name in a different manner from Americans. A person's surname is referred to as his "title" or "first name" because he is born with it. The Christian name is called the "last name." When a woman marries she assumes her husband's "first name" as her "title." For example, if Mildred McKinney marries John Davis, her "title" becomes Davis, her "first name" remains McKinney, and her "last name" remains Mildred.

117

Husband and wife use "last names" in referring to or calling to each other. When alone, however, the wife can use names to indicate the nature of the relationship she has with her husband or how she feels about him at the moment. If she loves him she calls him by his "title"; if she does not, by his "last name." Even if she loves him but is angry about something, she calls him by his "last name"; if she is pleased, she calls him by his "title." However, in everyday situations, when they are alone, they are apt to call each other "Daddy" and "Mamma"; in this case they have taken over terms used by their children in addressing them. When they are making love she may call him "Daddy" and he may call her "Baby." After the first child is born she may call him the "old man," both when they are alone and with others. (In order to avoid confusion, from this point on the "title" or "first name" will be referred to as the surname and the "last name" as the name.)

Father—Child. A father spends very little time during the day with his children; he is either working in the fields or at a bar talking with his friends. Since he frequently leaves the island to work, there are long periods when he is not at home. Because of this frequent absenteeism, he cannot become the main disciplinarian in the household. However, when he is home, he plays with the children. Both fathers and mothers prefer to play with girls, who were also reported to be the better-liked. Children do not develop strong emotional feelings toward their fathers. Nevertheless, a man will often speak of his "Daddy" in affectionate terms and will be proud to own and operate a boat or a shop that belonged to him. Furthermore, father-son rivalry does not seem to develop. The only cultural recognition of this is found in the belief that "if the child favors [resembles] the father, he will have to kill a chicken and throw it to him or they will row." This is interpreted by informants to mean that when the boy is five or six years old, the father will give him a chicken of his own to raise.

Mother—Child. Since the mother is constantly with the children, she not only provides for their immediate needs but also becomes the chief disciplinarian. Thus strong emotional ties, based on dependency and authority, develop between mother and child. Mothers claim they "punish" themselves in trying to raise and support their children, and therefore they say that their children should love them because they have "suffered" so. Thus mothers are provided with a rationale for their attempts to establish obedience and loyalty. This loyalty finds expression in several ways. If the mother and father "row," the children always take their mother's part; and if a fight develops, they will help her beat their father rather than try to separate their parents. I was unable to record a single case in which the children had assisted their father. This strong loyalty between mother and children continues throughout their lives. It finds expression through gifts, often money, to the mother. Of course, there are some exceptions. Children, especially boys who go to Nassau or the United States, may "forget their mothers," but it is usual for children to send presents to their mother, particularly when she becomes a widow and is no longer able to support herself.

The relationship between a girl and her mother is especially close. One of the sermons at the "turning out" service for the wedding described in Chapter II provides an interesting expression of this relationship. The sexton attempted to establish the precedence of the husband-wife bond over the mother-daughter bond. The congregation refused to help him complete the argument; they insisted that the daughter should help her mother rather than her husband. Moreover, this belief is illustrated in actual situations. Women who had been married for years told me that since they can be more sure of receiving help from their mothers than from their husbands, they will aid their mothers in preference to their husbands. Another example which brings out

119

this loyalty is the hymns chosen by girls at wakes: nearly every one of them will have the word "mother" in the title.

Brother—Brother. The relationship between brothers is usually characterized by companionship and cooperation, although as boys they will occasionally fight. As adults, if they are close in age and grew up together, and still live near each other, they will assist one another in work, drink together, and visit each other's homes. However, there are no cultural rules that say brothers must live near each other or cooperate economically. Although brothers may work together as adults, as boys they do not form work groups under the supervision of their father or the eldest brother. The absence of such groups stems from the fact that adolescent males are required to do little work. This is surprising, for boys frequently perform hard work in many agricultural communities throughout the world. Yet teen-age boys in Long Bay Cays are not asked to accompany their fathers to the fields on non-school days. Apparently adults feel that boys will soon enough have to work hard to support their families, and since agricultural techniques are simple, a long training period is not required for them to learn farming. The absence of a family work group means that the eldest brother does not have control over his younger brothers. Brothers are thus able to relate to each other on equalitarian terms, and since there is no prescribed behavior between them they can choose to make their relationship as close or distant as they wish.

Although an older brother does not supervise the work of a younger brother, terminological distinctions are made between the two. A boy calls all his older brothers "Bulla" or "Bulla (name)" and all his younger brothers by their name or a "pet name" (nickname). Parents sometimes call their eldest son "Bulla." The term seems to imply respect for age but little more. Since the Bahamas have always followed the law of primogeniture, the term "Bulla" may have at one time been a means of designating the one who is to inherit. But since in most families there is little valuable property to inherit, there is now no reason for terminologically distinguishing the eldest son on these grounds. Nor is the eldest son selected to receive his father's name, although it is the custom to name one of the sons after the father. Since most parents think they will have several sons, it is not usually the eldest son who receives his father's name.

Sister—Sister. The relationship between sisters is closer than that between brothers. Although this may result in part from the close ties girls have with their mother, it also results because girls assist each other in domestic chores. This work is performed under the direction of the eldest daughter, who is called "Tita" by the members of the household. The term is one of respect which carries the connotation of "the boss." Even people outside the household are apt to recognize her position by calling her "Tita." The next eldest daughter is called "Sister." The youngest daughters are called by their names or "pet names." The strong tie between sisters, which is based on affection and cooperation, continues throughout their lives. Sisters, if they live near each other, will look after each other's children. Thus sisters' children are more likely to be closer than brothers' children. The expression "two sisters' children" is used more frequently than "two brothers' children." This coalescence of affection, cooperation, and authority in the females of the household is also found in British Guiana (R. T. Smith 1956: 152-53). Cumming and Schneider (1961: 499) have referred to such clustering as "gynefocality."

There is a difference both in structural position within the terminological system and in meaning between the terms "bulla" and "tita." "Bulla," since it is used by a boy for any older brother, is an ego-oriented term; "tita," since it is used by all members of the household and occasionally by others, is a term designating a particular status or position in the domestic group. As has been pointed out, the latter term denotes authority, the former only respect. The terms appear to have different meanings because they reflect different types of status within the household. Thus, despite the rule of male primogeniture, the first daughter is the most important child, and this is expressed through kinship terminology.

Brother—Sister. The relationship between a brother and sister, although it may involve much affection, is considered to be one of protection and assistance. If the sister is older than the brother it is likely that she has helped to rear him, and thus he becomes indebted to her in much the same way that he does to his mother. Since he owes her a great deal, he is expected to help support her if this should become necessary. On the other hand, if the brother is older, he should look after his sister's welfare. One way is to protect her from being physically abused by other children. He may also shield her from the advances of undesirable suitors. When he is older he is expected to contribute financially to the rearing of his sister if necessary, and once she is married he sees that her husband properly provides for her. If her husband cannot do this the brother ought to assist in her support. The set of expectations described here is that of females rather than males. Since men believe that they owe their first allegiance to their wives, sisters tend to be jealous of their sisters-in-law. One female informant expressed this jealousy in the following manner: "My brother's wife owes me respect because she got something from me, and I got nothing from her." This means that now her brother is looking after his wife and not his sisters. In actual practice, however, brothers contribute little to their sisters' welfare because the money they earn must be used to provide for their wives and children. Still, if a sister is in desperate need, she may legitimately call upon her brother for assistance and will probably receive help.

Stepfather—Stepchild. What are believed to be the relationships between children and their stepparents have been described in Chapter III, where it was argued that the existence of these beliefs caused people who were entering new unions to leave their illegitimate children with their parents. A point to be considered here is the kind of relationship in those few households that contain a stepfather and a stepchild. Although the data are limited, informants are probably correct in saying that a stepfather treats his stepchildren well. His relationship to them will probably be like that with his own children. He does not have to punish them —a situation likely to cause a quarrel with his wife—since the husband is not the chief disciplinarian. An incest taboo becomes established between a stepfather and stepdaughter, and also with any of the latter's sisters not living in the household. Children call their stepfather "Daddy," and he calls them by their names. A stepmother and a stepchild so rarely live in the same household that no statement can be made about the relationship.

Half Sibling—Half Sibling. The relationships between half siblings resemble those described for siblings. Children of the same father, unless they grow up together in the same household (this is not likely to happen, since men do not bring children of a former union to a new union), are unlikely to be close friends, largely because they may never have had the opportunity to know each other well. Uterine siblings, particularly sisters, because of the close tie to the mother and the likelihood of growing up together, have much the same relationships as full siblings. If stepchildren with different fathers and mothers (i.e., children not biologically related) grow up in the same household, sibling ties are established between them, including the creation of an incest taboo. Although such "siblings" are expected to assist each other in the above-described ways, since they do not have the same mother they are unlikely to aid each other when they become adults.

123

This analysis of step- and half-relationships shows that the relationships between non-biologically related individuals who are members of the same household are virtually identical with the relationships which exist between cognates who live together. In other words, membership in a corporate group (Murdock 1960: 4) rather than consanguineal bonds creates relationships. This point will become clearer after an examination of the relationships between members of three-generation or grandparent households.

RELATIONSHIPS WITHIN THE GRANDPARENT HOUSEHOLD

An illegitimate child who is being reared in a grandparent household calls its grandmother "Mamma," its grandfather "Daddy" (if he is a member of the household), and its mother "Aunty" or by her name. Whether or not its mother is living at home makes no difference in the terminology. The child is treated by its grandmother as if it were her own child and by its mother like a younger brother or sister. However, the child learns at an early age who the real mother is, since no attempt is made to conceal her identity. Since the grandmother may very well have children of her own who are younger than her grandchild, the child will behave like an older sibling towards its aunts and uncles and call them by their names. On the other hand, if the uncles and aunts are older they will be called "Bulla," "Tita," or "Sister." The use of these terms and the relationships usually persist even after the child becomes an adult.

The presence of outside children in a household alters the relationships which otherwise would exist between kinsmen. Since terms of address are not only an integral part of a relationship but also express its nature, the above terminology indicates that relationships exist between particular kinsmen which would not occur if they were members of nuclear-family households.

124

If the child is living with its father and its father's parents, the father will be called "Daddy," the grandfather will be called "Daddy (name)" or "Papa," and the grandmother will be called "Mamma." Since the father-child relationship is not close in the nuclear-family household, the relationship of the child with its father does not differ much if they are members of a grandparent household. Since the relationships are essentially the same in the two types of households, the terminology is the same. The reason for the existence of different terms for father and grandfather is not to differentiate between different types of relationships, but to enable the child to distinguish between the two when he is with them.

This analysis substantiates the point that household membership, rather than genealogical ties, establishes the particular types of relationships which exist between kinsmen. In some cases, biological relationships will even be terminologically denied.

Consanguineal Relationships Outside the Household

Grandparent—Grandchild. The relationship between grandparents and grandchildren, except in three-generation households, is characterized by mutual affection. Grandparents are usually called "Grandma" and "Grandpa." The grandfather may also be called "Papa" or "Dada," terms not often used for one's father. Although the grandchildren usually live near only one set of grandparents, if it becomes necessary for the child to differentiate terminologically between the two sets of grandparents because they are frequent visitors to the home, then names will be attached to the "grandma" or "grandpa." Since a child hears its grandparents being called "Mamma" and "Daddy" by its own parents, the child is apt to use these terms but attach the names in order to establish the differentiation. Similar conventions are used in addressing great grandparents. Grandparents call their grandchildren by their names. (The third descending generation is referred

125

to as great-grandchildren and the fourth descending generation as "grinnie-gran" children.)

Uncle and Aunt—Nephew and Niece. The relationships of children with their uncles and aunts show great variability. A mother's sister is apt to be like a mother to the child because of the closeness between sisters. However, the child's relationship with his uncles and other aunts will depend in great part upon the type of relationship the child's parents have with their siblings. Ideally uncles and aunts have the right or duty to discipline nephews and nieces, but in actuality they do not exercise this right, unless authorized by the child's parents, for fear of disrupting their relationships with their siblings. The failure to perform this duty probably also derives from the fact that the uncle or aunt is related to only one of the child's parents. The other relationship is one of affinity, which, as has already been pointed out in the case of sisters-in-law, involves jealousy. Thus a sister will probably not discipline a brother's child for fear of creating conflict with its mother. Children call their parents' brothers "Uncle (name)" and their parents' sisters "Aunt (name)," and the uncles and aunts call their nephews and nieces by their names.

Cousin—Cousin. Two siblings' children are "first cousins." A first cousin and a child of a first cousin are "second cousins." The children of first cousins are "third cousins." A third cousin and the child of a third cousin are "fourth cousins." In other words, cousins are not described as being once or twice removed. This terminology, however, is not used to describe relationships, since exact genealogical connections are used to trace degrees of kinship. For example, a person would not say, "He is my second cousin," but rather, "He is my mother's sister's daughter's son." The number of degrees of consanguinity determines the feeling of closeness or distance between two relatives, i.e., the fewer the degrees, the closer the consanguineal bond is felt to be. Occasionally two people are related to each other through both their father's and mother's relatives. Such a relationship is called "double family." The kinsmen feel closer to each other because they can trace their genealogical connection through two routes. For example, if two siblings marry two siblings their children are not only first cousins but also "double cousins." Such a relationship is believed to be almost as close as the sibling relationship. "Double uncle" and "double nephew" also occur.

The rights, duties, privileges, and restrictions between cousins are similar despite the wide range of degrees of consanguinity possible between any two kinsmen. Since the kindred is exogamous, i.e., two related individuals cannot marry or have sexual intercourse, any kinsman may chaperon a young female relative. Although a mother usually takes her daughter to dances, she will permit any male relative to be her escort provided she is sure that he will keep close watch over her. Any relative, theoretically, can discipline a younger kinsman but seldom does so, for fear of offending the child's parents. He usually merely reports the bad behavior to the child's mother or separates the children if they are quarreling. An example was given in Chapter III: the woman who stopped the schoolgirls from bullying an outside child was related to all of them.

The relationships between cousins show great variability. If they live near each other they may become very good friends; in fact, if they are of the same age they may become closer than brothers. On the other hand, they may never meet, and furthermore, if they are distantly related they may not know of the consanguineal tie between themselves. In Chapter II we saw that a boy has to check his genealogy with his parents to be certain that he is not related to the girl he wants to marry. In addressing each other the young cousin calls the older person "Cousin" or "Cousin (name)"; in turn the older cousin calls the younger person by his name or a "pet name." The spouse of a cousin is also addressed in the same manner. The term "Cousin" denotes respect for age.

The members of a man's kindred, which of course includes all his cousins, are expected to try to prevent his becoming involved in fights. Any kinsman should stop a fight between two of his relatives. If he is related to only one of the men, he will try to stop that man. Kinsmen of the other man will try to hold their relative. However, if the two fighters are related and if their relatives want and expect to see one of the men beaten, they are likely to let the fight proceed. If the two men fighting are not related, any one of three things can happen. Relatives may pull them apart, as occurred at the fight at the wedding described in Chapter II. Or kin of each may say, "Let them fight." If both sets of relatives are in agreement, the fight will proceed. But if only one side wants the fight, a general brawl may start, with several men involved.

Kinship systems based on bilateral kindreds, of which the one just described is a case in point, permit consanguineal relatives to form the kinds of relationships that they want with each other, provided they are not members of the same household. In other words, the kinship bond may or may not be used as a basis for friendship. If two persons want to be friends, the consanguineal tie gives them a starting point on which to build a relationship. But if they do not wish this, there are no sanctions or mechanisms to bring them together and force the relationship upon them. This seems to result from the fact that kindreds are ego-oriented networks of kin or "categories of cognates" (Freeman 1961: 202-03), rather than corporate groups. Since corporate units involve individuals performing activities together, leadership and authority emerge. Thus the relationships between members become structured to the extent that rights and duties supported by sanctions control the behavior of the individuals. The kindred has no such structure, and therefore relatives can choose the way they want to act toward each other without having to fear that sanctions will force them to alter their behavior.

Societies with kindreds may also be characterized by unrestricted descent groups or descending kindreds (Otterbein 1964b: 32). Such groups are composed of all the descendants of one person. If the land and property of a person are left to all his descendants, generation after generation, there exists a landholding, unrestricted descent group. In contrast to personal kindreds, these groups have an authority system, since after the original owner dies someone is needed to administer and allocate land to his descendants. Thus relationships based on rights and duties come into existence. Since there is usually more than one household on the land, these relationships will extend beyond the individual household. In this way, the members of several households belong to one corporate group.

Groups with this structure are found in the Bahamas. Although a group of this kind is unnamed in Long Bay Cays, the land which it holds in common is called "generation property" and is under the direction of an "executor." "Generation property" comes into existence when a man leaves a will naming all his male and female descendants, generation after generation, as his heirs and his eldest son as the "executor." The will usually states that the land is never to be sold and that the executor can appoint his successor. The executor is considered to be a powerful person who can provide plots of land to any of his father's relatives in any manner which he chooses. Since the population is sparse and there is no shortage of land in Long Bay Cays, a person has no difficulty in being able to exercise his right. In fact, siblings' descendants of the original owner and affinal relatives, who have no actual rights, may be allowed to live on the land rent-free (Otterbein 1964b: 32-33).

These unrestricted descent groups are unimportant in Long Bay Cays because there are only ten households on four plots of "generation property": five households are on one plot, three on another plot, and one each on the remaining two plots. The first two executors have some control over the members of the other households on the generation property they administer. Although these groups are unimportant in this community, it is clear that the presence of generation property and the resulting unrestricted descent groups may be important in structuring relationships between distantly related kinsmen who live in different households. Such landholding groups may be more important in other villages on Andros or on other islands in the Bahamas. They are, for instance, important in Jamaica (Clarke 1953; 1957: 33-72; Davenport 1961: 447-454) and Barbados (Greenfield 1960).

AFFINAL RELATIONSHIPS

Parent-in-law—Child-in-law. A husband should show mild respect toward his parents-in-law, but otherwise there is no required behavior. He calls his mother-in-law "Mother" and his father-in-law "Father," or "Papa" if he is close to him. His relationship with them will probably be cordial, especially if they live in different villages. But sometimes there is animosity between them, which usually results from the son-in-law's being in a quasi-dependent situation. As pointed out in Chapter II, the husband may be living near his in-laws because they furnished the land on which he built his house. If this is the case, they will probably periodically expect assistance from him—either money or labor—which he may not want to give. If he does not assist them, they will think he is failing to fulfill his duty; on the other hand, he will believe that he is doing a great deal for them by supporting their daughter. Animosity thus results in part from the absence of culturally prescribed norms for regulating the relationship.

This animosity may also have another result. Since the wife lives near her parents she can readily call upon them for aid if a quarrel occurs between her and her husband. In fact, the proximity of her parents may make her more willing to express and exercise her desires. If a row starts, the mother-in-law invariably sides with her daughter; the father-in-law is likely to stay away so as not to be drawn into the dispute. If a fight develops, the mother and daughter will both attack the husband. In extreme situations the husband will even be driven away permanently. This occurred in one case described in Chapter III.

On the other hand, a daughter-in-law usually has good relationships with her husband's parents. She calls them "Mother" and "Father" and they call her by her name. A man's wife may become like a daughter to his mother. This may result because a woman's own daughters have moved away and the daughter-in-law tends to take their place. Also the birth of a child brings the mother and grandmother close together in caring for it. Not only does the grandmother help in looking after her grandchild, but the daughter-in-law may at times care for the youngest children of her mother-in-law.

Sibling-in-law—Sibling-in-law. The relationships between brothers-in-law and sisters-in-law show a great range of variability. In general, if they are close in age they are likely to be friends. However, it has been mentioned already that the relationship between sisters-in-law may be strained because of divergent expectations over how much assistance the brother should provide his sister. If their ages differ appreciably, the young in-law shows respect. This is shown in terminology: a brother-in-law can be called either "Brother-in-law," "Brother," "Bren-law," or "Bren"; a sister-in-law can be called either "Sister-in-law," "Sister," or "Sis." The older in-law calls the younger by his or her name. These relationships and this terminology extend to in-laws linked by two marriages, i.e., the spouses of two siblings (Otterbein 1964c). Since a father gives house lots to his sons, they are likely to live near each other, and thus their wives may become good friends.

A man should not have sexual relations with a sister-in-law, and I did not find any instance of such relationship. Probably it

131

does not happen, since a wife is permitted to have sexual relations only with her husband, and a husband would not seek out his wife's sister for a sexual partner, for he would most likely be refused and the knowledge of the request would be conveyed to his wife. In general, sexual relations between in-laws do not occur, because of their socially disruptive nature.

Affinal relationships, as with consanguineal relationships outside the household, are amorphous unless the in-laws live near each other and interact frequently. The context within which the interaction occurs molds the relationship: if there are factors promoting solidarity, they will be good friends (e.g., mother-in-law and daughter-in-law); if there are factors producing stress, they will feel animosity toward each other (e.g., son-in-law and parents-in-law, if he lives on land they gave him).

FICTIVE KIN RELATIONSHIPS

The godparent-godchild relationship is considered by the inhabitants of Long Bay Cays to be of importance to the child because it provides him with "relatives" who will at times assist in his upbringing. Anglicans and Baptists appoint godparents for their children at their christenings; the Anglicans insist that the godparents be members of the church, though the Baptists do not. There are two godfathers and one godmother for a boy and two godmothers and one godfather for a girl. Although official appointing of the godmother occurs at the christening, she is selected several months earlier at the ninth-day ceremony called "putting out the baby." Seldom does anyone turn down a request to be a godparent. In fact, one man has more than twenty godchildren. The head schoolteacher is the only person who receives so many requests that he finds it necessary to refuse most of them. Since godparents give presents such as clothes and food to their godchildren, parents choose people they think will help the child. This, of course, is the reason the schoolteacher receives many requests. Sometimes a relative is chosen, possibly even a sibling of the child. Occasionally a person will offer to be a godparent.

Although godparents are expected to care for the child as its parents would, if necessary, I know of no cases in which godchildren are being raised by their godparents. They should and usually do give presents to their godchildren, and they have the right to discipline them. The godmother, who is more important than the godfather, is supposed to give the child a Bible and a hymnbook, and to teach the child the Lord's Prayer and the Ten Commandments. In turn, the godchild must carry wood and water for the godmother, and also at times help her clean and wash. The godchild is expected to perform errands for the godfather. The godparent-godchild relationship also implies that when the child becomes an adult this pattern of reciprocity should continue. Thus godparents and godchildren frequently exchange goods and services.

Godparents and godchildren call each other "Godfather," "Godmother," "Godson," and "Goddaughter." A godmother may also be called "Gordy." The terms are apt to be expanded to include the person's name, e.g., "Gordy (name)." These terms take precedence over all other terms, even if the godparent is a sibling. They can also be applied to the spouses of one's godparents, for these individuals become drawn into the system of reciprocity. So do the children of one's godparents, called "Godbrother" and "Godsister." Since they are likely to be older than the godchildren, they call the godchildren by their names. A child and his godbrother or godsister do each other favors. Godparents and godchildren, as well as godbrothers and godsisters, are prohibited from marrying or having intercourse. Hence godbrothers, like cousins, can chaperon their godsisters.

Godparent-godchild relationships, like the ties between cousins, show great variability. At one extreme is the man with more than twenty godchildren who cannot remember who they all are;

at the other a man who visits his godmother nearly every day and helps her tend bar although she lives in another village. In other words, the relationship is one that can be used as the basis for establishing a close friendship. Since some people, particularly men, have many godchildren, it is impossible for them to develop close ties based on reciprocity with them all. Nevertheless, within the functioning of the kinship system godparenthood plays an important role, for it is an institution by which friends of the child's parents can become fictive members of the child's kindred or by which relatives can be made to feel a closer kinship tie to a younger kinsmen. Furthermore, if the members of nearby households are selected to be godparents, the neighborhood, which is composed in part of unrelated individuals, is converted into a quasi-kin-group.

In summary, the analysis of interpersonal relationships has shown the important role that the household plays in structuring relationships, both in their behavioral and their terminological aspects. Nearly every important relationship of an individual is with persons who are or have been members of the domestic groups to which he does or did belong. Sometimes, however, the individual has important relationships with the members of nearby households, particularly if they are parents, siblings, or in-laws. Occasionally the individual will have a close tie with a person, often a fictive relative, who lives in another village but with whom he interacts frequently. The analysis has shown that frequency of interaction, which is largely determined by residential propinquity, is more important than genealogical connections in structuring interpersonal relationships.

From the point of view of the community, rather than that of the individual, the type of relationship system just described produces a social system in which households and sometimes clusters of households are the functionally significant groups. Each domestic group would to a large extent function as an isolated unit if it were not for the fact that individuals usually maintain some of their relationships with former household members.

Chapter VI

Conclusion

THE ANALYSIS of the mating system of the inhabitants of Long Bay Cays has focused on the economic and demographic factors which are determinants of that system. These factors together produce a two-choice mating system, which itself is the major factor influencing household composition, i.e., household types and their frequency. These domestic groups structure the relationships between household members; to a large extent an individual's behavior toward his relatives, and theirs toward him, is determined by his placement within the domestic system.

The community of Long Bay Cays expects every young man and woman to marry, but to do so a man must be able both to support his wife and to provide her with a home. Many parents would refuse to grant permission for their daughter to marry if the man has not completed the building of a house. Nevertheless, he can become engaged to the girl while his house is being built. During the engagement he may go "on the contract," and in two or three years save enough money to complete the construction of the house. Even though the girl may become pregnant, this occurrence does not necessarily result in an earlier wedding. Marriage and the acquisition of a house are so esteemed that even couples who have been mating extra-residentially for several years do not begin living together prior to marriage. Therefore, consensual unions for young people are eliminated from the mating system.

As in many societies, women outlive men in Long Bay Cays; therefore there are more widows than widowers in the population. Many of these widows remain single, not only because of the shortage of widowers, but also because of their wish to remain in charge of a household and not lose their dower. Some men move in with widows and establish consensual unions; other men, usually those who are married, mate extra-residentially with them. According to the double standard of sexual behavior, married men must have love affairs and mate extra-residentially. The women they mate with are female household heads who are usually widows. Even though it is difficult to measure the frequency of extra-residential mating because of the secrecy of such affairs, we can be fairly confident that most female household heads have such relationships, for they need financial aid to manage their households.

The analysis of household composition has demonstrated that the mating system is largely the determinant of household types and their frequencies. A high percentage of early marriages, in the absence of extended family households, produces a high percentage of nuclear-family households. Girls who bear children to men other than their future husbands leave their children to be raised by their mothers or other consanguineal relatives when they marry or go to Nassau to work, thereby changing their parents' or relatives' nuclear-family households into grandparent households. Mortality and separation also produce shifts in household types. In a nuclear-family household, death or permanent absence of the husband creates a single-female or mother-child household; death of the wife produces a single-male or father-child household. In a grandparent household, death of one of the grandparents establishes either a grandmother or grandfather household.

Household groups play a salient role in structuring relationships, for an individual's most important ties—both in their affectional and jural aspects—are with the members of his household. Nevertheless, other consanguineal, affinal, and fictive relatives may be of importance if the individual regularly interacts with them, residential propinquity being the most important factor in producing frequency of interaction.

137

The analysis of the influence of economic and demographic factors on the mating system of Long Bay Cays has shown that high wages, saved to build houses, in conjunction with a surplus of women who mate extra-residentially are the two most important determinants of the mating system. This interpretation is supported by a comparison of Long Bay Cays with three other communities which have a two-choice mating system—i.e., a mating system characterized by marriage and extra-residential unions but not consensual unions. Incidentally, these are the only communities which I have been able to find from among numerous studies of New World Negro family organization that have such a mating system. All four communities have low percentages of consensual unions and high frequencies of extra-residential mating as measured by illegitimacy rates.

On Carriacou, a small island in the Lesser Antilles, 6 per cent of the conjugal unions are consensual unions (M. G. Smith 1962a: 227). St. Helena, on the Sea Islands off the coast of South Carolina, appears from Woofter's brief account of their family organization and the accompanying tables to have no consensual unions (1930); however, there probably were some which the investigator failed to observe or to note. Nevertheless, his account seems adequate enough for inferring the existence of a two-choice mating system. A third community with a low percentage of consensual unions is East End, Grand Cayman, one of three islands off the northwest coast of Jamaica. I have analyzed the unpublished census reports collected during the summer of 1962 by I. R. Buchler and found that only 2 per cent of the conjugal unions were consensual. The percentage of consensual unions in Long Bay Cays is nine. All four communities are characterized by extra-residential mating: their illegitimacy rates—Carriacou, 41 per cent (Smith 1962a: 239); St. Helena, 30 per cent (Woofter 1930: 207); East End, 32 per cent; and Long Bay Cays, 32 per cent

—are a clear indication of the high frequency of extra-residential unions.

These four communities have in common an important geographical and economic feature. They are on small islands situated a short distance from either the United States or a large West Indian island. Their location not only engenders a maritime way of life but also provides access to countries where jobs are available. Therefore many of the men find employment at sea or as migratory wage laborers. The money they earn is used primarily to build homes in preparation for marriage. This house-building requirement is present for Carriacou (Smith 1962b: 114), East End, and Long Bay Cays, and can be inferred for St. Helena from the occurrence of neolocal residence (Woofter 1930: 206).

The male absenteeism which arises from the excellent opportunities for employment produces a surplus of women, as indicated by the sex ratios of each community (sex ratio is computed by dividing the number of females by the number of males): Carriacou, 1.92 (Smith 1962a: 226); St. Helena, 1.26 (Woofter 1930: 266); East End, 1.18 (official census, April 1960); and Long Bay Cays, 1.10. Women who are unable to find spouses establish their own households and mate extra-residentially; female-headed households constitute 59 per cent of the households in Carriacou (Smith 1962a: 227), 32 per cent in St. Helena (Woofter 1930: 280-81), 35 per cent in East End, and 28 per cent in Long Bay Cays. In conclusion, the generalizations derived from an analysis of the family organization of Long Bay Cays appear to hold true for other communities that have a two-choice mating system.

References

Bahamas: Report for the years 1956 and 1957.
    1959   London: Her Majesty's Stationery Office.

Beckwith, Martha
    1929   *Black Roadways: A Study of Jamaican Folk Life.* Chapel
           Hill: The University of North Carolina Press.

Bell, Major H. MacLachlan
    1934   *Bahamas: Isles of June.* New York: Robert M. McBride and
           Company.

Buchler, I. R.
    1962   Unpublished Field Notes.

Clarke, Edith
    1953   "Land Tenure and the Family in Four Communities in
           Jamaica," *Social and Economic Studies,* 1, no. 4:81-118.
    1957   *My Mother Who Fathered Me: A Study of the Family in
           Three Selected Communities in Jamaica.* London: Ruskin
           House.

Crowley, Daniel
    1956a "Tradition and Individual Creativity in Bahamian Folktales."
           Ph.D. dissertation, Northwestern University.
    1956b "Boom and Bust in the Bahamas," *The Caribbean,* 9:221-224,
           230, 239-240, 253.

Comming, Elaine, and David M. Schneider
    1961   "Sibling Solidarity: A Property of American Kinship," *American Anthropologist,* 63: 498-507.

Davenport, William
    1961   "The Family System of Jamaica," *Social and Economic
           Studies,* 10: 420-454.

Dawson, W.
    1960   *A Mission to the West India Islands: Dawson's Journal for
           1810-17,* ed. A. Deans Peggs. Nassau: The Deans Peggs Re-
           search Fund.

Edwards, Charles L.
    1895   *Bahama Songs and Stories.* Memoirs of the American Folk-
           Lore Society 3.

Farquharson, Charles
    1957   *A Relic of Slavery: Farquharson's Journal for 1831-32,* copied
           from the original by Ormond J. McDonald, with an Intro-

duction by A. Deans Peggs. Nassau: The Deans Peggs Research Fund.

Fassig, Oliver L.
1905 "Climate of the Bahama Islands," *The Bahama Islands,* ed. George B. Shattuck, pp. 111-125. New York: The Macmillan Company.

First Research Corporation
1958 *Survey of Levels of Living in the Bahamas and Other Areas.* Miami.

Firth, Raymond and Judith Djamour
1956 "Kinship in South Borough," *Two Studies of Kinship in London,* ed. Raymond Firth, pp. 33-63. London School of Economics monographs on Social Anthropology 15.

Forsyth, E. W.
1929 "Andros," *Reports of the Out Island Commissioners for the Year 1929:* 14-18. Bahamas Out Island Administration Publication.
1930 "Andros," *Reports of the Out Island Commissioners for the Year 1930:* 8-15. Bahamas Out Island Administration Publication.
1931 "Andros," *Reports of the Out Island Commissioners for the year 1931:* 4-12. Bahamas Out Island Administration Publication.

Fortes, Meyer
1958 "Introduction," *The Development Cycle in Domestic Groups,* ed. Jack Goody, pp. 1-14. Cambridge Papers in Social Anthropology 1.

Frazier, E. Franklin
1939 *The Negro Family in the United States.* Chicago: The University of Chicago Press.

Freeman, J. D.
1961 "On the Concept of the Kindred," *The Journal of the Royal Anthropological Institute of Great Britain and Ireland,* 91, part 2: 192-220.

Government of Bahamas
1872 *Blue Book.* Nassau: *Nassau Guardian.*
1881 *Blue Book.* Nassau: *Nassau Guardian.*

1901 *Report on the Census of the Bahama Islands ... 1901.* Nassau: *Nassau Guardian.*

1911 *Report on the Census of the Bahama Islands ... 1911.* Nassau: *Nassau Guardian.*

1921 *Report on the Census of the Bahama Islands ... 1921.* Nassau: *Nassau Guardian.*

1931 *Report on the Census of the Bahama Islands ... 1931.* Nassau: *Nassau Guardian.*

1943 *Report on the Census of the Bahama Islands ... 1943.* Nassau: *Nassau Guardian.*

1954 *Report on the Census of the Bahama Islands ... 1953.* Nassau: *Nassau Guardian.*

Greenfield, Sidney M.

1960 "Land Tenure and Transmission in Rural Barbados," *Anthropological Quarterly,* 33: 165-76.

Henriques, Fernando

1953 *Family and Colour in Jamaica.* London: Eyre and Spotiswoode.

Herskovits, Melville J.

1941 *The Myth of the Negro Past.* New York: Harper and Brothers.

King, Charles E.

1945 "The Negro Maternal Family: A Product of an Economic and a Cultural System," *Social Forces,* 24: 100-104.

Landy, David

1959 *Tropical Childhood.* Chapel Hill: The University of North Carolina Press.

Leach, E. R.

1961 *Pul Eliya: A Village in Ceylon.* Cambridge: Cambridge University Press.

McKinnen, Daniel

1804 *Tour Through the British West Indies, in the Years 1802 and 1803, Giving a Particular Account of the Bahama Islands.* London: for J. White by R. Taylor.

Mitchell, Carleton

1958 "The Bahamas, Isles of the Blue-Green Sea," *National Geographic Magazine,* 113: 147-203.

Mooney, Charles N.
1905 "Soils of the Bahama Islands," *The Bahama Islands,* ed. George B. Shattuck, pp. 147-181. New York: The Macmillan Company.

Mosely, Mary
1926 *The Bahamas Handbook.* Nassau: *Nassau Guardian.*

Murdock, George P.
1960 "Cognatic Forms of Social Organization," *Social Structure in Southeast Asia,* ed. G. P. Murdock, pp. 1-14. Viking Fund Publications in Anthropology No. 29.

Murdock, George P., *et al.*
1961 *Outline of Cultural Materials.* New Haven: Human Relations Area Files.

Newell, Norman D., *et al.*
1951 *Shoal-water Geology and Environments, Eastern Andros, Bahamas.* Bulletin of the American Museum of Natural History, 97: 1-29.

Northrop, Alice R.
1910a "Bahaman Trip, General Notes," *A Naturalist in the Bahamas: John I. Northrop,* ed. Henry F. Osborn, pp. 1-24. New York: The Columbia University Press.

1910b "Flora of New Providence and Andros." *A Naturalist in the Bahamas: John I. Northrop,* ed. Henry F. Osborn, pp. 119-211. New York: The Columbia University Press.

Otterbein, Keith F.
1959 "Setting of Fields: A Form of Bahamian Obeah," *Philadelphia Anthropological Society Bulletin,* 13: 3-7.

1963a "The Household Composition of the Andros Islanders," *Social and Economic Studies,* 12: 78-83.

1963b "Marquesan Polyandry," *Marriage and Family Living,* 25: 155-59.

1964a "The Courtship and Mating System of the Andros Islanders," *Social and Economic Studies,* 13: 282-301.

1964b "A Comparison of the Land Tenure Systems of the Bahamas, Jamaica, and Barbados," *International Archives of Ethnography,* 50: 31-42.

1964c "Principles Governing the Usage of In-Law Terminology on Andros Island, Bahamas," *Man,* 49: 54-55.

Parsons, Elsie Clews
   1918 *Folk-Tales of Andros Island, Bahamas.* Memoirs of the American Folk-Lore Society 13.
Parsons, Talcott
   1949 "The Social Structure of the Family," *The Family,* ed. R. N. Anshen, pp. 173-201. New York: Harper and Brothers.
Peggs, A. Deans
   1959 *A Short History of the Bahamas.* Nassau: The Deans Peggs Research Fund.
Powles, Louis Diston
   1888 *The Land of the Pink Pearl.* London: S. Low, Marston, Steark, and Rivington.
Puckett, Newbell Miles
   1926 *Folk Beliefs of the Southern Negro.* Chapel Hill: The University of North Carolina Press.
Rawson, Sir Rawson W.
   1864 *Report on the Bahamas for the Year 1864.* London: G. E. Eyre and W. Spottiswoode, For H. M. Stationery Office.
Richardson, J. Henry
   1944 *Review of Bahamian Economic Conditions and Post-War Problems.* Nassau: *Nassau Guardian.*
Schoepf, Johann David
   1911 "Voyage from St. Augustine to the Bahama Islands," *Travels in the Confederation, 1783-1784,* trans. and ed. Algred J. Morrison, Philadelphia: Wm. J. Campbell.
Sharer, Cyrus Jewell
   1955 "The Population Growth of the Bahama Islands," Ph.D. dissertation, University of Michigan.
Siebert, Wilbur H.
   1913 *Legacy of the American Revolution to the British West Indies and Bahamas: A Chapter out of the History of the American Loyalists.* Ohio State University Contributions in History and Political Science I.
Smith, M. G.
   1962a *West Indian Family Structure.* Seattle: University of Washington Press.
   1962b *Kinship and Community in Carriacou.* New Haven: Yale University Press.

Smith, R. T.
  1956 *The Negro Family in British Guiana.* London: Routledge
       and Kegan Paul Limited.
Solien, Nancie L.
  1959 "The Consanguineal Household among the Black Carib of
       Central America." Ph.D. dissertation, University of Michi-
       gan.
  1960 "Household and Family in the Caribbean: Some Definitions
       and Concepts." *Social and Economic Studies,* 9: 101-106.
Statute Law of the Bahama Islands, The
  1799- Revised edition by B. H. Bliss in 6 vols. Published by the
  1957 Government of the Colony of the Bahama Islands.
Warner, W. Lloyd, Marchia Meeker, and Kenneth Eells
  1960 *Social Class in America: A Manual of Procedure for the
       Measurement of Social Status.* New York: Harper and
       Brothers.
Woofter, Jr., T. J.
  1930 *Black Yeomanry: Life on St. Helena Island.* New York:
       Henry Holt and Company.
Wright, James M.
  1905 "History of the Bahama Islands, with a Special Study of the
       Abolition of Slavery in the Colony," *The Bahama Islands,*
       ed. George B. Shattuck, pp. 419-583. New York: The Mac-
       millan Company.

Appendix

CENSUS OUTLINE

1. Who lives here? For each member of the household:
   Name
   Sex
   Age
   Birth status if child under fifteen years of age:
      Illegitimate or Legitimate?
   Relationship to all other members of the household.
   Conjugal condition: Single, single mother, married, widow or widower, separated, or consensual cohabitation.
   Marital residence (from what village?).
   Number of months per year spent here?
2. Whereabouts of absent children, aged fifteen and under, for women of the household?
   Name, names of parents, sex, age, birth status, living where and with whom?
3. Length of conjugal union?
   Number of previous unions, length, and marital residence?
4. How did you get this land and house?
   Land: bought, inherited, gift, rent, or generation property?
   House: built, bought, rent, inherited, or loaned?
   Description of house:
      Limestone or wood?
      Shingles or thatch?
      Presence of porch? (If yes, wooden or cement?)
5. What do you own?
   Houses, land, shop, bar, club, vessel, dingy (including property in Nassau)?
6. What is the occupation of adult members?
7. Have you gone on the contract?
   When, how many times, how long, how old were you?
8. What organizations do you belong to?
   Specific names? Are you an officer?

The procedure followed in utilizing the census outline was to interview one or more of the adult members of the household whenever

146

possible. However, since many men, and sometimes their wives and children, are often away from Long Bay Cays, I frequently had to interview close relatives of these persons. Thus data on twenty-three households, of a total of eighty-five, were collected indirectly. It is unlikely that this had any influence on reliability, except for ages, because the data were obtained from a primary relative of one of the adult members of eighteen households; the data were collected from a secondary relative for the remaining five. Each census report was examined for completeness and adequacy several times before I left Long Bay Cays. Wherever the data were not clear I revisited the household or interviewed a close relative. Topics for which I might have been given incorrect information, such as illegitimacy or consensual unions, were checked with reliable informants. For example, villagers I knew well were questioned about the birth status of children I thought might be illegitimate.

Index

Aboriginal population, 2

Affair. *See* Extra-residential union

Agriculture: eighteenth and nineteenth centuries, 3, 6; slash-and-burn technique, 3, 24, 25, 26-27; division of labor, 11, 14, 95-97, 120; provides subsistence, 23; fields, 24; laborers in the U.S., 24; tools, 25, 26; comparison of present and historic, 26. *See also* "Contract, The"; Cotton; Crops; Guinea corn; Indian corn

Andros Island: geography, 1-2; first settlements, 6, 9-10, 14; population, 6, 10, 12

Bahama Islands: climate, 1; geography, 1; population, 21; wedding festivities, 51, tory, 2-6

Barbados, 130

Bars: locations, 17-18; work in, 30, 97, 134; attendance, 80; ownership, 113

"Beau-stag," 56

Bell, H. M., 4, 6, 11

Bluff, The: location, viii, 8, 17; school, 18; population, 21; wedding festivities, 51, 54, 55; wattle-and-daub houses, 86

Boats: "smock-boat," 28; ownership, 113

Book of Common Prayer, The, 48, 53

Buchler, I. R., 138

Burial: societies, 17, 66; of child, 66. *See also* Society hall

"Bush," 24

"Bush medicine," 60

Carriacou, 138-39

Cat Cay, 31

Cat Island, 3

Caul, 64

Census: villages taken in, viii, 21; procedures, 13, 146-47; criteria, 21-22

Chaperon, 38, 44, 127

Children: steal fruit, 27; importance to adults, 56, 74; infant, 62, 65; chores, 95; residence, 107-10; relationships with parents, 118, 119, 123; relationships with siblings, 120-22, 123-24. *See also* Illegitimate children

Churches: location, 17, 18, 51; sanctions against premarital pregnancy, 43; functions, 54-55, 132. *See also* Wedding

Clarke, E., ix, 103, 130

Clothing, 89. *See also* Wedding

Club, 17, 113

Community, 18

"Conga People," 9

Congo Town: location, viii, 8, 16, 17; first settlers, 9; buildings in, 17-18; population, 21

Conjugal condition, 72-73, 91. *See also* Consensual union; Divorce; Extra-residential union; Marriage; Separation; Widows

Consanguineal family, vii

Consensual union: frequency, 81-82, 136; reasons for, 81-83, 136-37; role in mating system, 83-84, 138; in census-taking, 147

"Contract, The": men go to the U.S., 31; frequency of enlisting, 31; money saved, 31, 34, 136; in terminating engagements, 41

Cotton: plantations, 2; decline of production, 3, 6

"Cotton Islands": plantations on, 2-3; land given to ex-slaves, 5; crops, 24

Courtship: visiting girl, 33, 37; obtaining permission, 33, 37-39; meeting girls, 36, 38-39; role of parents, 36-38; practices in past, 37; taking girl out, 38; violation of patterns, 38-39. *See also* Chaperon; Engagement

Crooked Island, 3

Crops: comparison of present and historic, 24; grown in southern Andros, 24; listed in Farquharson's journal, 24; technical names, 25; planting and harvesting, 25, 26. *See also* Agriculture; Cotton; Guinea corn; Indian corn

Crowley, D., vii, 6

"Crown land," 9, 24

Cumming, E., 121

Dances: held in villages, 18; dance in Motion Town, 38-39; at wedding festivities, 47, 50, 51-52, 53-54, 55; types danced by bride and groom, 50; place to find sexual partner, 67

Davenport, W., 130

Dawson, W., 5

Delivery: effect of intercourse on, 58; place of, 60; pain experienced, 61; care of child, 61-62; midwife's tasks, 61-63; placenta, 62-64; care of mother, 63; umbilical cord, 63-64; resumption of duties after, 66

Descent groups, unrestricted, 129-30

Developmental cycle of households, 115-16

Division of labor, 11, 95-98, 117, 120, 121

Divorce, 68

Djamour, J., vii

"Double family," 126-27
"Double-luck," 57
Double standard, 67, 80, 137. *See also* Virginity
Dower, 91, 136
Dowry, 33, 34
Drigg's Hill: location, viii, 8, 17, 18; school in, 18; population, 21; girl from, 38-39
Duncombe Coppice: location, viii, 8, 17, 20; buildings in, 18; participates in events with Motion Town, 18; population, 21

East End, 138-39
Economic factors, influence on mating system, x, 136, 138-39
Edwards, C. L., 1
Eells, K., 111
Endogamy, 36
Engagement: ring, 33, 38, 39; letter, 33, 38, 39, 40; sexual intercourse during, 33, 42, 44, 58; house built during, 33-34, 136; termination of, 40-41; length, 44. *See also* Pregnancy
Enuresis, 89
"Executor," 129
Exogamy: kindred, 34-35, 127; village, 35, 36
Extra-residential union: establishment, 67-68, 100; married individuals, 69-71, 137; unmarried individuals, 77, 136; role in mating system, 83-84, 138-39
The Exumas: plantations on, 3, 4; population decline in nineteenth century, 5; home of ex-slaves, 5, 6; migration to Andros, 9, 14

"Families," 36
Farquharson, C., 3, 24
Fassig, O. L., 1
Fighting: husband and wife, 34, 74, 119, 131; men, 54, 128; wife and "sweetheart," 68-69, 70; children, 75-76, 120; as influenced by kinship, 128
First Research Corporation, 32
Firth, R., vii
Fish, 28-29
Fishing: economic importance, 23-24, 27-28; techniques of, 27-29; performed by, 95, 96. *See also* Sponge fishing
Folk tales, vii
Food: diet, 24, 27, 28, 98-101; at wedding festivities, 49, 55; preparation, 88, 95-98; meals, 98-99; costs, 99-100
Forbes Hill, 9
Forsyth, E. W., 6, 11, 12
Fortes, M., 90

Frazier, E. F., vii
Freeman, J. D., 128
Fresh Creek, vii
Furniture, 34, 87-88

"Generation property," 129-30
Godparents, 65, 66, 132-34. *See also* Relationships
Grand Cayman, 138-39
"Granny child," 66
Greenfield, S. M., 130
Guinea corn, 3, 24
"Gynefocality," 121

Henriques, F., ix
Herskovits, M. J., 6
High Rock: location, viii, 8, 17; considered unfriendly, 18; population, 21; location of wedding, 51-54
Households: headship, vii, 80, 89-92, 93, 106, 139; in research, ix, x; types, determinants of, x, 101-2, 137; determinant of interpersonal relationships, 124-25, 134-35, 137; types and frequency, 21, 89-90, 102-6; developmental cycle, 90-91, 94-95, 103-5, 115-16; economic features, 95-101, 111-16; composition, 104-11; residence of illegitimate children, 108-11; relationships within, 117-25
Houses: construction of, 3-4, 17, 33-34, 85-86, 111-12; nineteenth century, 10-11; role in mating system, 33-34, 43, 71-74, 81-82, 136, 139; lots for, 85, 92; types, 86-87, 112-13; rooms and furnishings, 87-89; ownership, 93-94
Hurricanes, 17, 85, 86

Illegitimate children: mothers of, 36-37, 41-77; rates of, 43, 75, 138-39; establish adult status, 56; attitudes toward, 75-76; reared by, 75-79, 137; naming, 76-77; residence of, 102, 108-11, 116, 124-25; in census, 147
Incest taboo, 123, 127
Income, nineteenth century, 10. *See also* Agriculture; "Contract, The"; Fishing; Sponge-fishing; Wages
Indian corn, 24, 25, 26
Inheritance: by illegitimate children, 75; of houses, 94-95; primogeniture, 120-21
In-law relationships. *See* Relationships
Intercourse: during engagement, 33, 42, 44; desire for, 57; positions, 58; during pregnancy, 58-59; postpartum, 66; premarital, 67; extramarital, 67; widows, 80; between in-laws, 131-32. *See also* Extra-residential union

Jamaica: family, ix; descent group, 130

"Jitney," 75. *See also* Illegitimate children

Kindred: structure, 34-35, 126, 128; exogamous, 34-35, 127
King, C. E., vii
Kinship. *See* Kindred; Relationships

Land: purchased in nineteenth century, 24; ownership, 24, 92, 113, 129-30; for house, 85. *See also* "Crown land"
Landy, D., 117
Law: statute, 39, 41, 46-47, 49, 68; illegitimacy, 41, 75, 76
Leach, E. R., ix
Liquor, heavy consumption, 11. *See also* Fighting; Wedding
Long Bay Cays: description, 14; population, 18, 21-23
Long Bays: location, viii, 8, 15, 17; buildings in, 18; population, 21
Long Island: plantations on, 3; population decline in nineteenth century, 5; home of ex-slaves, 5, 6; migration to Andros, 9, 14
Loyalists, 2, 5, 6
Lucayan Indians, 2
Lumbering, 6

McKinnen, D., 3, 11
Male absenteeism: reasons for, 12-13, 14; formula, 13; forces agriculture on women, 14; money saved, 23-24, 33-34; rates, 31; role in mating systems, 139. *See also* "Contract, The"; United States; Wages
Marriage: slave, 4-5; preparations, 33-34; mate selection, 34-37, 41; of cousins, 35; arranged, 37; ages, 44, 45, 47; duties of spouses, 53, 55; permanance, 74; mothers of illegitimate children, 77; remarriage, 79-80; frequency, 80; role in mating system, 83-84, 136. *See also* Divorce; Houses; Relationships; Separation
Mastic Point, 6
Maternal family, vii
Mating system: effect on household types, x, 101-2; determinants of, x, 136, 138-39; based on marriage and extra-residential unions, 83-84, 136-39. *See also* Consensual union; Extra-residential union; Marriage
Matri-centered family, vii
Matri-focal family, vii
Meeker, M., 111
Menstruation, 57-58
Midwife, 61-63, 65-66

Migration, 22-23. *See also* Loyalists; Male absenteeisms; Settlers; Slaves
Missionaries, 6
Mitchell, C., vii
Mooney, C. N., 3, 25
Morality, sexual, 36-37, 67. *See also* Double standard; Virginity
Mosely, M., 1, 5, 12
Mother-centered family, vii
Motion Town: location, viii, 8, 17, 19; buildings in, 17, 18; participates in events with Duncombe Coppice, 18; population, 21; scene of dance, 38
Murdock, G. P., 124
Murdock, G. P., *et al.*, 18
Music, band at dance, 51
Names: surnames, 117-18; used by husband and wife, 118; used for relatives, 120-21, 123, 125, 126, 127, 130, 131; used by illegitimate child, 124-25; used for fictive kin, 133. *See also* Illegitimate children
Nassau: fish market, 28; work in, 31, 32, 36, 78, 119; engagement rings purchased, 39; weddings in, 46
Nassau Guardian, 32
"Navel string." *See* Delivery, Umbilical cord
Negro family organization, vii, 138
Newell, N. D., *et al.*, 1
New Providence, 6
Nichols Town, 6
Ninth-day ceremony, 65-66, 132
Norms, statistical, ix
Northrop, A. R., 1, 6, 11

Obeah, 64
Occupations, 29-30, 96-97, 113
Otterbein, K. F., ix, 27, 90, 129, 131
Out-islands, 6
"Outside children," 75. *See also* Illegitimate children
Ownership: houses, 93-94; property, 113

Parsons, E. C., vii, 59, 65
Parsons, T., vii
Participant observation, viii
Peggs, A. D., 2
Plantations. *See* Agriculture; Slavery; Slaves
"Plantin' stick," 25
Population: Bahama Islands, eighteenth century, 2; Exumas, nineteenth century, 5; Long Island, nineteenth century, 5; Andros, eighteenth and nineteenth centuries, 6, 10; Andros, twentieth century, 10, 12; Long Bay Cays, 18, 21-23; analysis by age, 22-23; analysis by sex,

22-23; density, Andros, 24; analysis by household type, 104, 105-6
Post office-courthouse, 17
Postpartum care. *See* Delivery; Midwife
Pound sterling, 27
Powles, L. D., 5, 6, 9, 10
Pregnancy: premarital, 43, 44, 136; fertility, 56-57; knowledge of contraceptives, 57; beliefs about conception, 57-58; beliefs about pregnancy, 59; health of mother, 59-60; abortion, 60
Puckett, N. M., vii
Puerto Rico, 117

Rawson, R. W., 6, 10
Red Cross, 18
Relationships: determinants of, x, 126, 129, 131-32, 134-35; between parents and children, 78-79, 118-20, 123; between husband and wife, 117-18, 119; between siblings, 120-23; between kin, 124-30; between in-laws, 130-32; between fictive kin, 132-34. *See also* Households; Kindred; Names
Residence, marital, 35, 36, 85, 130-31
Richardson, J. H., 31
Rites: passage, 55-56; intensification, 56
Roads: construction, 4, 29, 95-97; location, 14, 17
Rolle, Lord, 5
Rolle Hill, 9
Rum Cay, 3

St. Helena, 138-39
Sanitation, 89
San Salvador. *See* Watlings Island
Schneider, D. M., 121
Schoepf, J. D., 11, 26
School, 18, 36
Sea Islands. *See* St. Helena
Separation, 56, 71-74, 137
Settlement pattern, 14, 17, 18
Settlers, English, 2
Sex ratio, formula for calculation, 23. *See also* Surplus of females
Sharer, C. J., 2, 3, 5, 6, 9, 13
Siebert, W. H., 2
Slavery, 2-5
Slaves: in Bahama Islands, 2, 4; from Africa, 2, 5-6; marriages, 4-5
Sleeping arrangements, 88-89

Smith, M. G., ix, x, 83, 138, 139
Smith, R. T., vii, ix, 55, 121
"Smock-boat," 28
Society hall, 50-51, 54. *See also* Burial
Socio-economic index, 111-16
Solien, N. L., vii, ix, 103
Southern Bight, viii
Spanish slave ships, 5
Sponge fishing: beds, 2, 12, 14; attracts men, 9-11; value of sponges, 10, 12, 24. *See also* Fishing
Staniard Creek, 6
Status, adult, 56
Surplus of females, 12, 23, 139

Telegraph station, 17
Transportation, 14, 17
"Turning out" ceremony, 50-51, 54-55, 119. *See also* Wedding
Twins, 64-65

United States, migratory labor in the, 13, 24, 30-31, 32, 34, 57, 119, 139. *See also* "Contract, The"; Male absenteeism

Virginity: valued, 41-42, 67; determination of, 42-43; symbols of, at wedding, 49

Wages: rates, 29, 31, 32; effect on economy of household, 90, 97-98, 99-100. *See also* "Contract, The"; Male absenteeism; United States
Wakes, 120
Warner, W. L., 111
Watlings Island, 2, 3-4, 24
Wedding: night, 42-43; clothing, 44, 47-48, 49, 50, 52; expenses, 44-45, 46; preparations for, 45-48, 49, 51; "The Marriage Banns Book," 46; dances, 47, 50, 51-52, 53-54, 55; bride "put away," 47, 51; participants, 48; procession, 48, 52; ceremony, 48-49, 52-53; reception, 49-50, 53; advice to couple, 50, 53; "turning out" ceremony, 50-51, 54-55, 119; functions of ceremony, 55-56
Widows: remarriage of, 79-80; household heads, 92,100-1, 136-37
Woofter, T. J., Jr., 138, 139
Wright, J. M., 4, 6